Charlotte I. Lee
Northwestern University

Oral Reading of the Scriptures

Houghton Mifflin Company / Boston
Atlanta Dallas Geneva, Ill.
Hopewell, N.J. Palo Alto London

Printed in the U.S.A.

Library of Congress Catalog Card Number: 74–11950

ISBN: 0–395–18940–3

Contents

Preface v

1 **The Basics of Oral Interpretation** *1*
The Interpreter as Communicator *3*, First Steps
in Getting at Meaning *4*, The Writer and
His Art *7*, Logical and Emotive Content *11*

2 **The Use of the Body and Voice** *14*
Using the Body *16*, Posture *18*,
Muscle Tone *20*, Gesture *21*, Empathy *23*,
Sense Imagery *26*, Improving the Voice *27*,
Breath Control *28*, Volume and Projection *33*,
Focus of Projection *35*, Pitch and Quality *37*,
Rate and Pause *40*, Intelligibility of Speech *42*

3 **Literary Style** *46*
Introduction *48*, Body *51*, Conclusion *52*,
Sentences *53*, Sentence Length *57*,
Syntax of Sentences *67*, Word Choice *71*,
Speech Phrases *77*, Prose Rhythm *79*

4 Narratives *83*
Point of View *87*, Action and Plot *89*,
Climax *90*, Time and Place *91*, Characters *93*

5 Narratives in the Old Testament *97*
Characters *98*, Setting *102*, Tense *103*,
Climax of Plot and Action *103*,
Narrative Style *105*

6 Narratives in the New Testament *110*
The Gospels *111*, Types of Narrative *113*,
Special Problems of the Narrator *116*,
Analysis of the Passion and the Death *118*,
The Acts of the Apostles *124*

7 Epistles *126*
Corinthians *127*, Galatians and Romans *130*,
Stylistic Elements *133*,
Special Problems for the Interpreter *138*

8 Poetry in the Bible *141*
Organization *145*, Word Choice *148*,
Parallelism *151*, Rhythm *153*

9 Lamentations *166*
Poem I *168*, Poems II, III, IV *171*

10 Prophecies and Revelation *175*
The Prophecies *177*, The Book of Revelation *185*

Index 192

Preface

This book is for anybody with some acquaintance with the Bible who finds that acquaintance pleasurable and the sharing of biblical reading with others a satisfying and challenging experience.

There has been no attempt here for exhaustive explanation for its own sake. The examination of details within the units selected for study is designed to increase the reader's and hence his listeners' awareness of the richness and vitality of the literature. The focus in the selections is on the familiar, which, because of its very familiarity, may have lost some of its original impact. This text is intended to be nondenominational in scope but essentially religiously oriented.

Some attention is given to the reader's use of his voice and body, since voice and body make up the twofold instrument through which we reach one another. The Bible, like all other great literature, must be read aloud to realize its full potential. Our voices serve us to achieve verbal communication with others, and our bodies give out equally important nonverbal signals to our listeners.

The chapters deal with the literary qualities that are characteristic of the various types of writing abounding within the Bible and with the fostering of a deeper comprehension and fuller appreciation of the literature when read aloud, whether for one's own pleasure or that of one's listeners. The approach, then, is to the demands of the page before us, not to what has always been said *about* that page.

Samples for analysis and discussion have been drawn from numerous versions, including the King James, The Torah, The Revised American, The Anchor Bible, The New English Bible and the Jerusalem Bible. They were selected for their literary interest. I am grateful to the publishers of these versions for their permission to quote from them.

This book is the direct result of the influence of many people to whom I am deeply indebted. The first of these people, paradoxically, are those who read the Bible as if it were a series of dead quotations. It is they who make one yearn to hear it read fully.

The second group is made up of all the intelligent and dedicated men and women I have had in my classes in the oral interpretation of the Bible, who, by their vitality and challenging questions, helped clarify my thinking on the relationship between the Bible and the spoken Word of God.

The third group to whom I wish to acknowledge my indebtedness is made up of colleagues who read the book in manuscript and offered invaluable suggestions for its development. These include Rev. Donald Cuzack, Niles College of Loyola University; Lowell G. McCoy, Hebrew Union College—Jewish Institute of Religion; Rex P. Kyker, Abilene Christian College; William E. McDonnell, University of Wisconsin at Eau Claire; Morris M. Womack, Pepperdine University.

1
The Basics of
Oral Interpretation

In the interest of clarity it is perhaps wise to remind the reader at the outset that the term *interpretation* has three generally accepted connotations. When the student of languages uses the term he usually means the transcription of one language into another. When the biblical scholar uses it he probably means a theological investigation and exegesis of a particular translation or version of the Old and New Testaments. We shall be using the term *interpretation* in its accepted sense as an academic discipline within the field of speech and will be referring to *oral* interpretation or the reading aloud of a literary text.

Oral interpretation is the art of sharing with an audience a work of literary art in its intellectual, emotional, and aesthetic entirety. This sharing is accomplished by a voice and body operating under a disciplined and informed mind that is cognizant of *all* the elements in the piece of literary art and the way they operate together to produce a total achievement. Thus, the interpreter is concerned with detailed literary analysis, techniques of vocal and physical projection, and control of response from his listeners. When you read the Bible you have at your disposal the world's greatest literature. Your audience is predisposed in its favor. You have a clear privilege and responsibility to do justice to both.

Throughout this book we will be using the terms *interpreter* and *reader* interchangeably, remembering that the reader does more than merely translate written symbols into sounds. In his performance he becomes the medium through which the written symbols reach the minds—and the emotions—of his listeners, whether they be a few friends or a formal audience.

The interpreter's art is re-creative. It is comparable to that of a musician playing the work of an artist-composer. He takes the symbols which have been put down on the printed page, and by thorough analysis, painstaking rehearsal, and strict discipline in the use of his body and voice, he revitalizes and reactivates the creative mind of the writer. He brings his own experience and insight and special knowledge to bear on the clues which the writer has given him. He then submits his experience and responses to the order imposed by the literary artist.

Like the language expert you as interpreter will be more or less concerned with translation problems (which we will touch on later). Like the biblical scholar you will become involved in theological evaluations and exegesis of difficult passages. But your primary interest will be in *sharing* a selected text with your listeners.

Oral interpretation shares with classical rhetoric an interest in *pronunciatio*, the proper handling of voice and body, and in *elocutio* which originally referred to effective literary style, as well as in *inventio*, the selection and arrangement of ideas. The difference between the two lies primarily in the fact that the interpreter is making use of the writings of another, and consequently the tasks of choice of literary style and arrangement of ideas have already been done for him by the author. It is your responsibility to discover all the elements the author has used and then bring your techniques of *pronunciatio* to serve them adequately in order to share the totality with your audience and to elicite the appropriate responses.

The Interpreter as Communicator

Oral interpretation is a vital part of the whole field of speech and thus of the complex and far-reaching modern concept of communication. All phases of communication must have four basic factors: a communicator, a message, a receiver or receivers, and the effect of the message as the receiver understands it, which takes the form of some physical, mental, or emotional response. Obviously these four factors operate in interpretation as well as in public address, homiletics, theatre and all the other phases of speech. But the interpreter must go beyond the usually accepted meaning of the term *message*. Indeed it is at this very point that too many people go astray when reading religious and biblical material. The message is there, certainly, but it is not always a simple, direct persuasion to overt or even primarily logical response. The interpreter's role is not merely to bring a message to his audience but to bring an experience that can be shared, since it is often his responsibility to set a mood or bring about a response that is primarily emotion centered.

The interpreter is concerned directly with all three phases of the field of communication: communication by written symbol, since he is using literature which has been put down in print; communication by spoken language as he presents the literature orally; and communication by visible or nonverbal language, i.e., gestures, facial expressions, muscle tone, empathy, and all the elements of bodily action which are visible to his audience and hence influence their acceptance or rejection of the experience he wishes to share. The first of these three phases, the communication by written symbol, has been taken care of by the author or authors. The second, communication by spoken language, and the third, communication by nonverbal language, are the direct responsibility of the interpreter. Obviously, the situation is complicated by the fact that there are really two communicators in interpretation: first the author and then the interpreter. These two must be in perfect accord, saying the same thing in the same way, for the listeners to receive the message and act upon it. If the author's message seems to conflict with the interpreter's, the listener is distracted and confused.

First Steps in Getting at Meaning

Scholars agree that much of the Bible was originally oral rather than written. Consequently, we have three influences at work in the written symbols: the mode, method, and meaning of the original speaker; the comprehension of the message by the author and his integrity in reporting it when he is not the original speaker; and the comprehension, integrity, and scholarship of the translator whose version has been selected.

In regard to the first influence, the singer or singers of the psalms, for example, or Jesus as the direct speaker in the parables reported in the New Testament, or Moses' words to the people, you must bring your knowledge of religious, political, and economic history, geography and social customs to bear on your examination of the printed page. Your reading of the chosen text will be enriched and clarified by whatever knowledge these other areas can give you.

It is not the intention of this study to enter into the modern controversy about authorship of the various books of the Bible, fascinating as that subject is. We shall accept the printed page of whatever version we are discussing as the basis from which to work toward a *literary* analysis. It would be absurd to spend time and space listing arguments to prove that the Bible is successful literature. It has been accepted as great literature for centuries. It only remains for the interpreter to do it justice.

In the case of the Bible we obviously have two complicating factors in discussing the total comprehension of the written symbols. The first, which concerns you as interpreter only indirectly, is the matter of translation. The original symbols, both oral and written, unfortunately do not mean much to many of us. Biblical scholars, however, have translated or transferred one set of written symbols into another, or to be exact into many others. One need only compare some of the modern translations which are now available to be aware of shades of meaning that vary with changes in word choice or syntax. Whatever you can learn of the original meaning of the words will sharpen your appreciation not only of some of the literary puns and acrostic psalms (which of course cannot be translated but which clearly indicate conscientious, careful workmanship), but also of some of the troubling passages and allusions and metaphors as well.

The interpreter's only problem in this area is choosing the translation that most completely suits his own literary and theological standards and the occasion for which the selection is to be used. The intended audience must certainly be considered regarding expectations and theological persuasions. But the interpreter's concern as he reads must be *finally* with the literary rather than the theological analysis of the selection. He brings to his analysis whatever theological principles he embraces plus sound knowledge of biblical and liturgical history and of the universality of human experience. He then moves into literary analysis, directing his techniques to interpret what he finds on the printed page.

The second complication concerns you the interpreter directly. It is the twofold problem of dealing with unfamiliar allusions and archaic references and, paradoxically, with familiar references. Often you need not explain obscure references specifically to your audience unless their comprehension of the total selection depends upon it. But you yourself must know, for instance, the importance of geographical references—cities of great power or arid desert lands—and of allusions to people and ceremonies that have historical or ritualistic connotations. Such awareness will enable you to give the proper emphasis and associational values to your reading. Another possible obstacle to a vital and compelling reading of the Bible is the practical need to break the books into fragments. This practice leads to neglect of the context from which the section was drawn and often obscures the obvious intention of the passage. There are innumerable examples of this problem throughout both the Old and New Testaments. When a fragment or section is used as a unit it must be kept in the context of the whole.

The other half of this twofold problem stems from the fact that your audience is probably already somewhat familiar with some of the material you are about to share with them and thus has numerous preconceived notions about how it should sound. However, the fact that your audience already knows "what it is about" means that you must use all of your knowledge and technique to make familiar passages vital and alive. The fact that certain faults, such as monotony of pitch and pace, and the "biblical tone," have always been present does not mean that they must be perpetuated. We will discuss this further in the brief chapter on the use of the voice and body in the interpretation of religious literature. We will be using some of the most familiar biblical passages as examples throughout the book.

If a selection is worth reading at all, it is worth the effort to see that it catches and holds the listeners' attention. It is in the area of recapturing the vitality of the Bible that there seems to be the greatest need for a fresh approach to the Bible as *literature*. Biblical research has concentrated so much on *what* is being said that the importance of *how* it is said has been all but forgotten. Many readers of scripture become so fascinated by footnotes and commentaries that they lose sight of the form the literature has taken.

The Interpreter and his Art

The Bible is made up of a myriad of literary forms. In later chapters we will turn our attention to some of the characteristics of these various literary forms and the way they manifest themselves in certain familiar sections of the Bible. Each form makes its own demands on the interpreter, and within the larger classifications of forms there are innumerable individual differences among the selections. We cannot approach a reading of religious literature with a narrow, stylized pattern of vocal and physical techniques nor with a mind content with categories. Each selection must be analyzed for what it contains in terms of organization, style, and allusions, for variety and contrast, climaxes, sound values, and dramatic elements. There is no one way to read religious literature.

Perhaps no other area of literature has greater need for both flexibility and control in making use of various schools of literary criticism. You must bring innumerable extrinsic considerations to bear on achieving total comprehension of your selection. Nevertheless, when you have chosen a translation or a version, you must be guided in your communication of that selection by what has been recorded on the printed page. Your own taste and your knowledge of history and criticism will influence your choice. But from then on you are committed to what you find before you.

In the definition of interpretation presented earlier in this chapter the word *art* was used twice. It is this duality of art that makes interpretation so challenging and satisfying to both reader and listeners. Art implies skill in execution. It demands discipline and training in the use of appropriate tools, intelligence, and experience, plus the ability to order these ingredients into a meaningfully controlled form.

Let it be clearly understood that art is the exact opposite of "arty" and "artificial." There is no place for exhibitionism for its own sake. The truest and finest art is disarming in its seeming simplicity and its ultimate totality. It makes its observers aware of the result, not the means, used to achieve that result. Technical display is not art. Art is the systematic application of knowledge and skill in effecting a desired result, which in the interpretation of biblical literature is the effective communication of the Word of God. It is the result of a preparation so thorough, painstaking, and sincere and a technique so perfectly coordinated with the demands of the material that the listeners cease to be concerned with the interpreter and concentrate fully on the literature itself. Implicit in the whole process of interpretation is a sincere and honest desire to share with an audience. Without this impulse to share there can be no vital communication.

The writer of a piece of literature is the creative artist. He orders ideas, words, sounds, allusions, and all the other elements of style into appropriate form. In the case of biblical literature the identity of the writer or writers has often been lost or questioned in the passing centuries. Nevertheless, someone took on the creative task, and our concern here is rather with the resulting order than with the individual himself. Moreover, we are faced with the question of varying translations and versions. Again we must remain faithful to what we find on the printed page. We may certainly exercise selectivity among the various versions, but having settled on a selection, our basic concern is with what has been put down and how it has been ordered and formed.

In our earlier discussion of the four basic factors of communication we mentioned the effect of the message on the receiver or receivers as taking the form of physical or psychological action or often both. Without this fourth factor the circle is not complete. For the message to have the desired effect the communicator must have a purpose in mind. To ascertain his purpose, the interpreter takes his cue from the author. He must examine the literature thoroughly for clues to the author's purpose and then bring his own thinking into line with the desired effect. Literature may be written to clarify, to instruct, to inspire, to exhort, to persuade, to praise, to comfort, to entertain, or to achieve a combination of two or more of these purposes. It may be primarily aimed at evoking a logical response or at the sharing of a basically emotional experience. Method of organization, choice of words and referential material, and use of tone and sound values are all clues to the author's intention and attitude and must be discovered and used by the interpreter to help achieve that purpose. In the New Testament, for example, a comparison of the Synoptic Gospels will indicate variations in the selection of details, reflecting each writer's preoccupation with different aspects of Jesus' personality and life, his resurrection, his teaching, his human qualities, his divinity, and so forth, as well as the particular position each writer held in relation to the early church itself and the problems it faced at different times and places.

The need to clarify purpose is probably at the core of the customary divisions of the books of the Old Testament into Law, History, Prophecy, and so forth. These categories are not of primary importance to the interpreter except as a general guideline. There are numerous overlappings and a wide variety of types of writing to be found within the large classifications. Moreover, you will probably be using only a segment of a book and your approach must be dictated by what you find within that particular segment, as well as within the context of the book as a whole.

As we have said, the writer of a piece of literature has already taken care of the problems of word choice and method of organization. They were the result of careful selectivity in order to best achieve the writer's purpose. It is imperative, then, that you find out how each detail works in the total selection and what you must do to make the selection achieve its total effect. This requires careful analysis of what the writer has given you to work with and skillful and unobtrusive use of your techniques of voice and body. Much of this book will be devoted to methods of analysis for the all-important literature of the Bible. Only after the literary analysis has been completed can you turn specific attention to vocal and physical techniques.

Logical and Emotive Content

The intellectual or logical content of a piece of literature is primarily "what it means." It is on this that the interpreter of biblical and religious literature brings to bear all his knowledge of theology and history, in order to explicate and clarify. Beyond the simple denotation or dictionary meaning of the words as they relate to each other there is the more complex matter of allusions and connotations which are often made more difficult because of changing modes and mores.

The emotive content evolves from that quality in the writing which arouses pleasure or pain and which stimulates the audience to reflection, hope, contentment, fear, joy, gratitude, or any emotion or combination of emotions. In its simplest concept it might be said to embrace the "how" of what is being said and grows directly out of the "why" it was said.

It must be remembered that logical content and emotive content are interdependent. The degree of their relative importance in any given selection will vary widely depending in part on the purpose of the original writing and the purpose for which it is being used with a modern audience: tradition or personal preference in rituals such as marriages, funerals, prayer and Bible services, for instance. Nevertheless, it is your responsibility to use everything you find in the selection and to exercise care that you are not violating or negating the totality which the author has given you.

Words seldom have meaning independent of connotative association or emotion-arousing qualities independent of intellectual association. Consequently, except for the process of analysis the emotional content and the intellectual content cannot be separated. You must find out exactly what has been written. You then allow yourself to experience it emotionally, relying on clues found in the writing. You bring your experience and your knowledge of human nature to bear on your response and then apply the test of relevance. Your personal and subjective response is legitimate only insofar as it is completely and clearly relevant to the clues you have been given. You then work with your voice and body so that you may share the total relevant response with your audience and elicit from them a corresponding response.

The aesthetic elements referred to in the definition of interpretation contain many of the above-mentioned clues. They are the aspects of literary art which make one treatment of a subject more successful and satisfying than other treatments of the same subject. It is with the aspects of literary art and the clues they provide for use of body and voice that this book is primarily concerned; the following chapters will reflect this emphasis in more detail.

As soon as all the written symbols and their relationships are completely understood the interpreter moves to the second and third phases: communication by spoken language and by visible or nonverbal language. Often during this phase of preparation he will experience a broadening and deepening of his first comprehension of the written symbols.

Although some may hesitate to agree completely with Marshall McLuhan that "the medium is the message," [1] the way in which an idea is expressed is certainly part of its effectiveness. McLuhan's interest of course extends

1. *Understanding Media: The Extensions of Man* (New York: McGraw-Hill, 1964).

from the printed page into other forms of media. Nevertheless the principle involved is an interesting one and partially applicable to literature, as well as to the interpreter who himself becomes part of the "medium."

It cannot be said too frequently that the oral interpreter is responsible for everything he finds on the printed page whether it be psychedelic typography, poetic structure, or archaic references, and his voice and body must transmit the total work appropriately. You cannot communicate what you do not know. Literature is not just something being reported. The way in which it is expressed is often its most important attribute. It is not enough to know what a selection is about. It is not enough to know what it means. You must also know *how* it means what it means. You must be aware of every technique at the writer's disposal so that you can accurately evaluate and use his principles of selectivity. Total knowledge of what and how and why are the only safe guides for your own techniques.

2

The Use of Body
and Voice

In Chapter One we talked briefly about the relationship of message, medium, and receiver or receivers. For the interpreter the message is found on the page of literature and is at the heart of his communication to the receivers. The medium, on the simplest level, is the arrangement of letter symbols on that page which, when carried to an informed and alert mind, translates into words with meaning and connotation. But the interpreter himself becomes a medium for the receivers. Through him the written symbols become sound symbols for them, and the full meaning of the message is conveyed through verbal and nonverbal clues. He communicates the message with all its associations through his body and voice which in turn are controlled by his mind.

This chapter will concern itself with a few simple suggestions for improving voice and body communication. Some of the material will be familiar to you but may serve as a convenient checklist for measuring the degree of control of your present techniques.

One of the problems we mentioned in Chapter One is the almost universal familiarity with some of the passages. Occasional practice on elemental techniques can be most helpful in retaining the freshness of that material. Even if you are reading the Bible aloud to yourself (and aloud is

the only way, incidentally, to read for maximum richness) or to one or more friends, some of the suggestions
that follow will increase your pleasure and effectiveness.
If you are sharing it with a group, some attention to your
techniques of communication is essential.

In the above paragraph the word *techniques* was used
repeatedly. For several decades this word carried with it
an implication of artificiality. Modern interpreters, however, have come to realize the necessity of voice and body
discipline. Technique may be described as the method
of procedure in creating an artistic work, as well as the
degree of expertise with which the procedure is carried
out. The finer the technique the less obvious it is and the
more it contributes to the totality of the art object or, in
the interpreter's case, the literature which he is reading.
Any display of physical or vocal virtuosity for its own sake
distracts from the material it should be supporting and is
considered in poor taste by modern audiences and certainly has no place at all in the interpreting of biblical and
religious material. It is the literature which is important,
and the modern interpreter uses his technique to communicate the literature; he does not use the literature as
a vehicle to display his technique. Such a display might be
interesting for a moment or two, as is an exhibition of
calisthenics or a recital of scales, but it would do violence
to the interpreter's purpose—which is to share a work of
literary art in its entirety.

Conscious attention to technique should be restricted
to the practice period. During performance the reader's
attention must be concentrated on his material and on
eliciting the desired response to that material from his
listeners. If preparation has been adequate, the muscles
will respond according to the habits instilled by practice.
As skill and experience increase, the habitual response will
become more natural and you will need only an occasional

practice session on technique to be sure you have not developed any mannerisms or tensions which might distract your audience or give them false impressions.

As a modern interpreter you will need to work on vocal and bodily technique as a musician practices scales, so that your muscles may respond without apparent prompting or effort. Only then can you hope to achieve a total response from your audience. Just as a musician cannot give a satisfactory performance without having first perfected the handling of his instrument, so you an interpreter, who is both instrument and instrumentalist, cannot do justice to the selection you have chosen unless you devote some attention to the proper use of body and voice.

Using the Body

It is a common mistake to assume that we communicate with others primarily through our voices. As a matter of fact, what we see is often more vivid than what we hear. Thus nonverbal language, or the *visible language of the body* can underscore or contradict what we are trying to convey by verbal or spoken language. In a given situation, it reveals our attitudes toward ourselves, toward those we are addressing, and finally toward the material we are attempting to communicate.

The interpreter whose attention is on himself and the impression he is making rather than on his selection and his interest in sharing that selection gives off clues that will alienate his audience. An audience is quick to resent a "holier-than-thou" facial expression, the "wiser-than-thou" posture and "more-inspired-than-thou" gestures. Likewise they are quick to question the authority of a speaker who seems unsure of himself. Sometimes these impressions are the result of habits which have been so firmly established that the interpreter is no longer aware of them. Although many religious speakers have been trained in just such pompous gestures, their ability to communicate is often hindered rather than enhanced because these gestures distract from the material and set up barriers to sharing.

From the moment the audience is aware of the physical presence of a speaker, they are making judgments and establishing a condition of mental and emotional acceptance or rejection. It is important that they be ready and willing to accept both the speaker and his material.

Bodily action may be defined as any muscular movement of the body. This movement may be a full gesture, or it may be merely the tensing or relaxing of the small muscles around the eyes or mouth or across the shoulders; or it may be a combination of any of these movements. It also includes the manner of sitting before one takes the stand, the approach to and departure from the platform, movements of the head, shoulders, arms, hands, torso, and legs, shifts in foot positions and balance, change of posture, facial expressions and muscle tone of the entire body.

An elaborate array of rules for posture and gesture is not needed by the modern interpreter. He knows that the test of effective bodily action is how it works in the communication and sharing of the material at hand. Nevertheless he must work for strength and for control. Too many speakers attempt to communicate from the neck up. Genuine sharing involves the entire body working as a unit to serve the material. Bodily action is effective when it is so unobtrusive as to go unnoticed except insofar as it contributes to total response and when it is free of distracting personal or habitual mannerisms.

Posture

The basis of effective bodily action is good posture which in turn is primarily a matter of proper positional relation between the parts of the body. Good posture is that arrangement of bones and muscles which results in perfect natural bodily alignment, each unit doing its appropriate job of supporting and controlling the body structure. Barring physical defects, good posture requires nothing more complicated than standing straight and easy from the ankle bone to the crown of the head so that the skeletal structure falls naturally into balance. This is not as effortless as it sounds, however, if bad posture habits have been allowed to develop.

Because the muscles of the body are easily trained and adjust themselves rather quickly, errors in balance may be firmly established without apparent tensions and strains, but they continue to exist. One of the most common errors in posture allows the spine to sway in at the center of the back. This causes the neck to be thrust forward and the pelvis to be tipped out of natural alignment in order to preserve balance. Such posture tightens the throat muscles, interfering with vocal flexibility, and tenses the muscles across the base of the ribs, inhibiting breath control. Sometimes compensation is effected by thrusting the chest forward; this posture encourages shallow breathing and places added strain on the delicate throat muscles. At the opposite extreme the spine is allowed to curve out so that the shoulders droop forward, the chest sags and the pelvis tips forward causing the stomach to protrude, thus crowding the important diaphragm muscles and cutting down on breath capacity.

The secret of standing straight is not the old familiar "hold your shoulders back" admonition of our adolescence. The shoulders should be held easily and naturally on top of the rest of the body. If the spine is straight the shoulders will tend to assume this position and the chest will lift slightly, causing the large muscles of the abdominal wall to be drawn in. Atop the neck column the head should be held in easy balance, neither protruding forward nor tilted back out of alignment. This is the basic position from which bodily action develops. Obviously you do not hold your head rigid, nor any other part of your body for that matter, but an occasional check on the crown of your head, shoulder balance and spine alignment will give you a balanced, flexible, responsive, and coordinated body.

A very simple and comfortable way to check on your body alignment is to lie flat on the floor (a bed is too soft and will conform to your habitual errors) and stretch as far as you can, pulling from your toes to the crown of the head. Relax your shoulders and arms and become aware of the part your feet must play in the coordination of your whole frame. Then, when you stand, force your muscles to remember the "all in one piece" feeling which you developed during the few minutes on the floor.

In his eagerness to reach his listeners, a speaker will sometimes develop the habit of leaning forward from the waist. Or he will emphasize a point by a thrust of the chin and/or shoulders. These postures make the listeners feel they are being pushed at and they will immediately retreat. The opposite extreme of bending back from the waist is equally alienating, as though the speaker were keeping as far as possible from his listeners. A too casual slouch suggests indifference and inhibits full control of breathing. These are all postures which have become habits with some speakers. They are all effective for certain passages on certain occasions, but they must not become so set as to be invariable.

Muscle Tone

Muscle tone refers to the degree of tension or relaxation present in the entire body. When the posture is good, the body is in a state of controlled relaxation with no undue muscular strain or tension. The properly poised body is flexible, responsive, coordinated, and fluid. It is "all in one piece." Controlled relaxation is not to be confused with apathy or lack of physical energy. The interpreter who looks as though he is too tired, depressed, or bored to stand up straight communicates a negative impression to his audience. Relaxation is an easing of tension; it is not total disintegration. The degree of relaxation is controlled in the interests of dignity and poise, and it is partly determined by the requirements of the material to be handled.

Muscle tone is affected by the mental attitude of the speaker as well as by his control of the physical aspects of posture. It will vary from obvious tension to assured, controlled relaxation in direct proportion to the interpreter's confidence in himself, in his material, and in his audience. Any performance will carry with it a degree of excitement which is translated into physical tension. The secret is to be able to channel that tension so that it becomes an asset instead of a liability. The "butterflies" in the stomach which indicate tension are not a sign of fear but of excitement. This excitement, if properly controlled and understood, communicates itself to the audience in terms of a vital, stimulating performance. Too frequently, however, the inexperienced performer attributes this tension to stage fright—and immediately sets up a fear pattern. If the material is acceptable and preparation has been adequate, then the "butterflies" are a good sign.

They are the result of excitement and involvement without which no performance can possibly succeed. Of course, if the interpreter has prepared inadequately and is really unsure of his ability, or is not sure that he has done the best he can, then there is no help or sympathy for him. He cannot hope to solve his problem until he is willing to put more time and effort into careful and complete preparation.

Gesture

A gesture may be defined as any clearly discernible movement which helps express or emphasize an idea. In the usual sense, gestures are overt actions limited to the hands and arms—and occasionally the head and shoulders. These parts of the body do not function as separate entities, however, but involve a "follow-through" which both affects and is affected by the degree of muscle tension of every other part of the body. Thus it is impossible to treat gesture apart from an awareness of posture and of muscle tone in general.

Unlike the reader who was trained in the theories and practices of the last century when books on "elocution" and "expression" devoted several chapters to detailed study of gesture, the modern reader is little concerned with gesture as a separate and specific part of his training. Rather, he believes that gesture is an integral part of bodily action and that it grows out of his responses to his material. It must aid in complete communication. If an action does not help communicate the material, it is not a gesture; it is only a distracting and extraneous movement which violates the basic principle that nothing an interpreter does should call attention to itself. This is not to say that gestures are not to be used. But their use must be dictated by the needs of the material being presented.

Whether an interpreter uses any gestures as such normally depends upon two considerations. The first, as we have said, is his material. The interpreter will use whatever bodily action is necessary to clarify meaning and to effectively convey emotional quality. He is attempting to create a total impression in the minds of his listeners and thus help them re-create what the author has put down. Too many or too specific gestures are likely to call attention to the person of the interpreter and hence distract from the material.

The second consideration in the use of gesture is the personality of the speaker. Some interpreters respond physically to their material with greater ease than do others. If gestures are difficult for you and make you self-conscious, forget about them and concentrate on empathic response and muscle tone. You should use whatever gestures you wish in practice until you can handle them effectively when you need them, but you should never let gestures become an issue when you are before an audience. When the interpreter's concentration shifts from his material to the problem of gestures, his audience will be quick to sense his preoccupation. If, on the other hand, you have a tendency to "talk with your whole body," use whatever gestures make you feel at ease and help you communicate your material. It is important, however, to keep in mind both facets of this advice—"make you feel at ease" and "help you communicate." There is the danger that gestures that make the interpreter feel at ease may distract his audience and thus actually block communication.

Perhaps the interpreter has developed certain habitual physical actions which are not gestures at all in the sense of helping to express the idea. He may be using a repetitious movement, such as a constant raising and lowering of one hand or a tilt of the head or a shrug of the shoulders. Unfortunately, religious leaders are some of the worst offenders in the matter of such "stock" movements. Under ordinary circumstances, it is inadvisable for the interpreter to work before a mirror because by doing so he is likely to divorce bodily action from its proper function of communication. If, however, he suspects that he has a too-regular pattern of movement, an occasional checkup before a large mirror will help call his attention to his fault.

As we have noted, the modern interpreter does not plan specific gestures. He never marks passages to remind himself to execute a carefully worked out movement at a particular place. Rather, he strives for such complete understanding of his material that he will be able to respond to it so fully that his gestures and muscle tone are an integral part of that response.

A good gesture conforms to no rules except the rule of effectiveness. It is effective when it helps to communicate, is unobtrusive, and does not result in distracting mannerisms. It depends upon and grows out of the reader's total response to the material. Like every other aspect of technique, gesturing must be the result of the reader's mental and emotional response to what is on the printed page. As such, it will be a powerful force in engendering corresponding responses in the listeners.

Empathy

One of the interpreter's subtlest and most powerful tools is his control and use of empathy. Although its roots are in classic Greek, *empathy* is a term borrowed from modern psychology. It is literally a "feeling into," that is to say, a projecting yourself into a work of art in order to identify with the mental—and thus emotional and physical—state of a person or persons within that work of art. This mental projection of oneself into a piece of literature implies, of course, emotional response to the writing as well as logical comprehension of it.

Every writer who deals with emotions to one degree or another, uses words and phrases that may cause some mental disturbance; his words may engender pleasure or pain, activity or repose. The interpreter responds to these phrases and words in his own mind and muscles as he prepares the material. If he has not precisely experienced what the author is describing or creating, he can usually recall some parallel or approximate situation which once evoked a comparable response. Emotional response and physical response are closely interrelated; one intensifies the other. As you respond mentally and emotionally to the written material, your muscles tighten or relax, usually without conscious effort. The tightening or relaxing of the muscles affects the tone of the entire body.

A word of warning is advisable at this point. The muscular response is in itself a result of inner or mental activity. The outward or physical signs are an indication of that inner activity, never a substitute for it. The mental and emotional response must come first; the muscular response must follow. Thus the first and basic step in empathy is the interpreter's full mental, emotional, and physical response to the selected piece of literature. Without this total response, the second step is impossible.

The second step in empathy concerns the audience's response to the interpreter's material. This response usually takes the form of an unconscious imitation of the speaker's muscle tone. When the interpreter is responding empathically to his material, he gives physical cues to his hearers, who in turn respond by muscular imitation. This muscular imitation helps intensify their emotional response. It is the same phenomenon which causes one to frown and feel depressed or irritated, to smile and feel happy, to yawn and feel tired or bored because someone else is frowning, or smiling, or yawning. A knowledge of this imitative aspect of empathic response is of vital importance to the interpreter. All too often we, as listeners, are robbed of the simple comfort or joy of some of the words of the Bible because what we see and imitate is a tone of pomposity or condemnation instead of quiet dignity and love of mankind.

The true interpreter will be aware of the value of empathy inherent even in the way he approaches the platform. During his introduction he will use it to help establish an emotional readiness in his audience. If his own emotional state of readiness for the selection's experience is complete, it will affect the tone of all his muscles. And the audience, by unconscious imitation of what it sees, will adopt the physical tone that makes it receptive to the emotional response which both the author and the interpreter are communicating. Psychologists have a complex scientific framework within which they study empathy, with varying theories to explain its source and effects. We as intererpreters, however, are primarily concerned with how it works in the delicate but basic problem of interaction of the literary selection with the interpreter who presents that selection and the members of the audience.

Finally, it should be noted that the current of empathy runs in both directions, for the reader in turn receives a stimulus from his audience. Thus, generated by the material on the printed page, the circuit of response is complete: from the material to the interpreter, out to the audience, and back again to the interpreter.

Sense Imagery

Much of our empathic response comes from imagery which appeals to our senses. The types of imagery are *visual*, appealing to our sense of sight, *auditory*, to our hearing, *tactile*, to touch, *thermal*, to heat and cold, *gustatory*, to taste, and *olfactory*, to smell. In addition there are two types of imagery which affect muscle response. They are *kinetic*, which pertains to a sweeping overt action, and *kinesthetic*, which pertains to muscle tension and relaxation and is thus closely related to empathy. The important thing to remember is that the senses seldom work independently of each other, and a word or phrase which appeals primarily to sight, for instance, will probably appeal to other senses as well.

For example, there is a strong empathic response and a kinesthetic tightening of muscle tone in the primarily visual imagery of "And when Aaron and all the children of Israel saw Moses, behold, the skin of his face shone; and they were afraid to come nigh him" (Exod. 34:30, King James). Another interesting example of complex imagery is found in Eliphaz's speech to Job:

> Now, I have had a secret revelation,
>   a whisper has come to my ears.
> At the hour when dreams master the mind,
>   and slumber lies heavy on man,
> a shiver of horror ran through me,
>   and my bones quaked with fear.
> A breath slid over my face,
>   the hairs of my body bristled.
> Someone stood there—I could not see his face,
>   but the form remained before me.
> Silence—and then I heard a Voice . . .
>   (Job 4:12–16, The Jerusalem Bible)

The imagery shifts rapidly but it is held in the unity of response to a situation which the interpreter must suggest through his body and voice. One need only imagine the effect the memory of this experience had on Eliphaz and his purpose in relating it to Job to know that it cannot be read as if he were saying, "Take my advice, Job."

Probably neither you nor your listeners have ever had a revelation such as Eliphaz describes, but the sensations in these four verses have been experienced by all of us to a greater or lesser degree. Your listeners probably will not be consciously aware of the physical manifestations of the response which you re-create but they will respond to your muscle tone, your voice quality, and your pace; the experience will gain in vividness as they share it with you, Eliphaz, and one another.

The Bible is full of such images, and we will consider them again when we discuss various types of writing in both the Old and New Testaments. For the moment it is enough to remind ourselves that all of our impressions and most of our basic knowledge have come to us through our senses, and writers use sense imagery in the form of description or comparison to sharpen our perception and make relationships more vivid. We must realize the images and respond to them fully to allow our listeners to receive their full impact.

Improving the Voice

In the preceding discussion we focused most of our attention on the development of a flexible, responsive body. From time to time, however, we touched upon the effect of bodily action on vocal technique. Body and voice are a twofold instrument, and the interpreter learns to control them both so that they combine perfectly to communicate whatever the literature demands. The body, as we have seen, makes its own special nonverbal contribution; but it is the voice, of course, which is basic to verbal communication, because unless the interpreter can be heard and understood, muscle response and appropriate gestures will be of little value.

The ordinary speech of most people is adequate for general conversation and for informal communication. But the oral interpretation of literature requires additional flexibility and special control. The fact that you use your speaking voice every day, and have done so since you were a child, is no guarantee that it is an adequate instrument for the satisfactory communication of difficult and demanding literature such as that found in the Bible.

Breath Control

The first concern of anyone interested in voice improvement should be breath control, because without it the production of good vocal tone is impossible. Proper use of the normal breathing mechanism is simple. Any difficulties are due to bad habits which may be the result of physical or psychological tensions. An understanding of the muscles involved in the breathing process and of the functions they perform may help locate and release some of these tensions.

In inhalation—the intake of air—the major concern is with the amount; in exhalation—the release of air—it is with control. The whole process of breathing rests on the basic physiological and physical principles of the balance of tension and relaxation in opposing sets of muscles that serve to control the creation of a vacuum.

When the diaphragm (the large dome-shaped muscle at the floor of the chest) *contracts,* it lowers and pushes downward against the *relaxed* abdominal muscles; thus the lengthwise expansion of the chest is increased. As this action is taking place, the muscles between the outer surfaces of the ribs contract, the rib cage is thus lifted and extended, and the side-to-side and front-to-back expansion of the chest is accomplished. This increase in size creates a vacuum inside the chest cavity. To fill this vacuum, atmospheric pressure forces air into the space, equalizing the pressure inside and outside the body. The air is forced down through the windpipe (trachea), on through the bronchial tubes, finally coming to rest in the flexible air sacs in the lungs, where the bronchioli terminate. The air sacs in the lungs inflate as the air enters, and when the lungs are thus extended the process of inhalation is complete. Obviously, then, breathing is an active muscle process.

When the mechanism is ready for the process of exhalation to take place (following the exchange of oxygen and carbon dioxide in the blood), the muscle fibers in the diaphragm relax, and the diaphragm rises in the dome-shaped position within the chest. The muscles on the outside of the rib cage relax as the ones between the ribs on the inside contract. This action pulls the extended rib cage inward. All this pressure upward and inward acts upon the elastic lung tissue containing the air forced in during inhalation; the elastic tissue begins to collapse, and the air is forced out of the lungs, up through the bronchial tubes, through the windpipe, and finally out of the nose or mouth. Thus one cycle of respiration is completed.

In exhaling for speech, however, there is frequently another action in addition to the relaxing of the diaphragm in the lower chest area. This action is the firm contraction of the abdominal muscles which are relaxed for inhalation. As they contract for exhalation, they support the action accomplished by the relaxing of the diaphragm, and in this way help to control the outgo of air.

It is simply an additional action, or rather a continuation of an action, in the process of exhalation during silent breathing.

Now, where should you begin your exercises so that you will have greater breath capacity and better control of exhalation? The first thing to remember is that proper breathing is possible only when the posture is good. If each muscle is to perform its assigned function, the body must be in a state of controlled relaxation—that is, in a state of nicely balanced relaxation and essential tension. Wrongly induced tension inhibits the flexibility of muscles that control the intake and the outward flow of air. One of the most frequent errors in breathing practice is forcing the muscles of the rib cage and the abdomen into a rigid position. These muscles must be firm, but they cannot function if they are locked. If the muscles below the ribs are "tucked in" after a full inhalation, they will be ready to help in the important functions of support and control.

In exercises for improving breathing habits, it is particularly important to have the spinal column erect but not forced into position, the shoulders level, and the muscles that support them free from tension. Strong lifting of the shoulders in inhalation serves only to put tension in the wrong area, with consequent damaging effects on the vocal tone.

A simple exercise to achieve the proper balance between tension and relaxation in the special muscles of respiration may be helpful. This exercise also tends to show *where* concentration of energy should be—at the "beltline" rather than in the throat.

1. Contract the abdominal muscles *sharply* and force the air out of the chest on a single vocalization such as "Ah- -h- -h," much as if sighing. Hold the contraction of these muscles an appreciable instant, then *suddenly*

release the tension. Notice that the air rushes into the chest and fills the lower portion (perhaps more) of the lungs upon the release of the tension. Exhale by forcing air out of the chest with the gradual contraction of the abdominal muscles as the diaphragm is relaxing and returning to its dome-shaped position.

2. Repeat the process described in step 1, and as the air rushes in on the release of tension in the abdominal muscles, make a conscious effort to lift the upper rib cage slightly (careful—*not* the shoulders!) so that more space is created in the upper chest, and the whole chest is well extended and can accommodate a large intake of air. The upper portion of the lungs should be filled now, as well as the lower. Exhale, pushing the air out with the relaxing of the diaphragm and the gradual contracting of abdominal muscles and lowering of the rib cage. (Don't collapse and let the shoulders sag!)

3. Repeat the process described in step 2. After you push out all the air, take another full, deep, easy breath. Now, as you start to exhale the full breath, begin to vocalize by counting aloud. As you begin to run out of breath for vocalizing, begin gradually to contract the abdominal muscles (*not* the upper chest ones) as you continue counting. You are now utilizing "forced exhalation." When you can no longer force air out of the chest by the strong but comfortable contraction of the abdominal muscles, stop the vocalized counting. Don't sacrifice a good quality of tone in the effort to "squeeze out" more sound. This will only result in undue tension in the upper chest and throat muscles—the very thing you want to avoid.

This is the basic exercise for developing good breath control and should be used as a starter for any period of exercise. You should not work steadily at this or any other exercise when you begin to feel tired. Until you grow accustomed to a new method of control or a marked effort to increase capacity, go back to your usual manner of breathing for a "rest." It should become increasingly clear, however, as you follow this type of exercise, that the sooner you can make this method automatic, the easier will be the whole breathing process.

As you are able to take in larger amounts of air with ease and continue forced exhalation to support the tone, you should be able to count more numbers on one breath. Try with each exercise period to increase the count, taking care always to avoid straining the throat, forcing the tone, or sacrificing good quality. Count at what seems an easy volume (loudness) for you, and at a pleasing level of pitch.

No experienced speaker will ever start to address an audience without taking a moment to get a full, easy, satisfying breath. This, of course, must be done subtly so that it does not call attention to itself. In the few seconds you spend waiting for your audience to settle and focus their attention, you can check on your posture and calm your nerves amazingly well with a full deep breath. Then inhale properly and you will be surprised at how much more relaxed and confident you feel.

The interpreter learns to breathe wherever the material demands a pause; he does not pause in order to breathe. It is usually impossible to get a capacity breath except in the major pauses that complete the units of thought. Therefore, the final step in control of breathing is to learn to inhale quickly and unobtrusively while still using the proper muscles.

Frequently a speaker inhales properly and uses his full breath capacity but still is unable to sustain a long flow of sound. Here the problem is not one of an insufficient supply of air but of inadequate control of exhalation. This is one of the major causes of "dropping" final words or syllables so that they do not carry to the last row of the audience. A simple exercise will help determine whether the control muscles collapse instead of exerting steady pressure as they relax:

1. Inhale a full, comfortable breath. Hold a lighted match directly in front of your lips as close as your profile will allow. Start to count aloud in full voice. You should be able to continue until the match burns down. If you blow the flame out, check the state of control of the muscles in and around the rib cage. Most of us exhale more than we need to on certain sounds, such as "*two*" or "*three*" or "*four*."

2. Light another match, take another deep breath, and repeat step 1, speaking very softly with conscious control of the rate of relaxation of the muscles involved. You will feel as though you may explode, but you won't, and you will be made aware of where the control must be exercised. As you gradually increase your volume to normal, you will find that the match will flicker but that you will not extinguish it by a sudden spurt of air.

Volume and Projection

These two inseparable factors in communication are so important that they must always be of utmost concern to the reader, actor, or speaker. Anyone who has been in an audience of any size and found to his distress that he could not hear the speaker knows the immense importance of sufficient volume and good projection. The interpreter's primary purpose is, after all, to communicate his material to his receivers. If he cannot be heard, he has obviously failed in his primary objective.

Actually, the terms *volume* and *projection* are sometimes used interchangeably, and indeed they are both part of the reader's ability to be heard and understood. For greater clarity in this discussion, however, let us consider volume as degree of loudness and projection as the act of directing the voice to a specific target.

Of course you must be able to make your voice fill the room in which your listeners are gathered. You must learn to control volume in order to fill that space easily without distorting your voice, or blasting down the back wall if space is limited. You must know how much volume is required and how to achieve the greatest possible flexibility within that requirement. Your knowledge of the entire breathing process is basic to your control of volume.

Most large churches or auditoriums are equipped with public address systems. These modern mechanisms can be a mixed blessing. Remember that they amplify your voice with all of its good and bad features. Too many people do not trust them and feel that they must shout over and past the microphone to reach their listeners. The best advice is to get someone to listen to you as you practice using the microphone and find the level which allows your voice to carry without distortion. Set the controls high enough so that you don't need to lean into the microphone at close range. If your voice is strong and full, allow yourself greater distance from the microphone. Some systems have directional microphones that pick up sound from one direction only. If this is the case, be sure you don't wander "off mike" when engaged in bodily action. Most systems, however, are nondirectional and will pick up from any angle, usually through the top of the microphone. Take a little time and learn to use whatever system you are confronted with.

Mere volume, however, is not always enough. It is, unfortunately, not unusual to encounter an amateur speaker who can be heard but cannot be understood. Obviously this touches on the problems of pronunciation and articulation, which will be considered later in this chapter. Being understood also depends to a degree on the speaker's control of projection.

The first requirement of adequate projection is sufficient volume to carry the tone to whatever distance the demands of material and situation make. The second requirement is the right mental attitude. This applies to the speaker with good control of volume as well as to the one who is less expert. For good communication, and hence projection, is a product not only of breath control but also of the speaker's constant awareness of his listeners. In other words, you must keep the back row of your listeners in mind and be sure that your words reach them. This advice is sound whether the audience is composed of a few people grouped around a fireplace or hundreds gathered in a church or auditorium. Your mental attitude toward communication has an indirect but observable effect on the physiological control of projection. Thinking of your listeners, wanting to be sure that they hear and share the full effect of the literature, you will tend to keep your posture erect and your head lifted slightly so that your throat is free from tension.

Focus of Projection

It is sometimes helpful to think of the voice as a tangible thing—a thing to be directed and tossed at a target. This trick of "throwing the voice" may smack of ventriloquism, yet it is a practice everyone uses at times. The child calling to attract the attention of his playmate down the street sends his voice down to him; the football fan shouting advice to the players on the field directs his voice without conscious thought to the exact spot where his attention is focused. When the adult is carrying on a conversation in a room full of people, he may project across the room to answer a remark or add his bit to a conversation over there. When he wishes to be confidential, he lets his voice drop, and his circle of direction narrows so that he fills only the desired area.

The following simple exercises for focus of projection can be practiced most effectively in a large room. They have been conceived primarily in terms of concrete situations, enabling you to concentrate on the volume and focus suggested.

1. You are seated at a desk in the center front of the room. You see a friend at the door; you call an easy greeting. He waves and goes on his way. You think of something you ought to tell him. You call his name quickly, but he apparently doesn't hear, for he keeps on going. Without leaving your seat, call again; have a good full breath as you start to call and direct the sound at his fast-disappearing back. Do the same thing again with more volume and longer sounds supported by forced exhalation. Be sure you catch him this time.

2. You are giving directions to a group of people on working out a diagram. The room is large, and everyone must hear. Direct your remarks to various places, thinking of certain people who might be there. After you have given instructions and the group starts to work, a question arises down in front. You shift your focus of projection, reduce your volume, and answer the person who asked the question. You then decide that others might need that special information, too. You raise your volume and expand your area of projection to attract

everyone's attention, then repeat to the group what you have said to the individual. As you do this, take care to direct your voice to various parts of the room so that all will hear.

3. Think of your voice as a ball which you can toss to various parts of the room. Aim it carefully at the far corner. Next let it drop onto the floor in front of you. Then send it with a strong thrust to another part of the room. Be aware of how your mind takes the aim which your voice follows. This is a useful principle to recall from time to time as you address a large or small group of receivers. Be sure they actually "receive" your message.

4. Until you get used to the feeling of supporting projection with the big muscles of the diaphragm and rib area, keep one hand on your midriff while you are doing these exercises. Put the other hand lightly on your throat. When you feel the throat muscles tighten, stop and start over making sure that the big muscles "bounce" the voice out. Wherever you are directing your voice be sure the push does not come from tightening your throat.

In working to develop volume and projection, you are concentrating on one of the basic requirements of all speech: that the audience be reached. Volume depends largely on adequate breath supply and proper support in exhalation. Projection combines these physical aspects with the phychological aspects of mental directness.

Pitch and Quality

Although pitch and quality are different attributes of sound, they are so closely related in the human voice that they may be considered together. The way the vocal bands vibrate basically determines both the pitch and the quality of the vocal tone—the pitch by the rate, the quality by the complexity of the vibration.

The *pitch* of a sound is the position of that sound on the musical scale. It is categorized very generally as high, medium, or low on the scale range. Skill in using pitch is of considerable importance to the interpreter in suggesting shades of meaning and in reflecting attitude. Changes in pitch lend variety and richness to the material being read and help to hold the attention of the audience. A change of pitch produces *inflection*, and a speaker's *inflection range* is the entire pitch span between the highest and lowest tone of which he is capable.

Any pattern in the variation of pitch levels results in melody. When there are no discernible changes of pitch, the result is a monotone. Melody is an asset to the interpreter, but it can also become a problem. Many individuals have in their ordinary speech a characteristic inflection pattern that becomes part of their personality. This is highly commendable, and it is certainly to be expected that some of that pattern will be carried over to their work before an audience. It often happens, however, that the reader's pattern is so marked as to call attention to itself and thus impede communication of the material.

It is very easy to develop a false pitch level that strains the throat and will in time cause fatigue and hoarseness. Sometimes in our youth we decide our voices are too high or too low, and we set out to change them. But instead of opening the throat so that the full set of vibrators can operate effectively, we push the voice down into the chest where it rumbles away on one or two tones, inhibiting both intelligibility and flexibility. Or, in trying to raise the pitch, we mistakenly tighten the throat muscles and speak from the back of the mouth instead of letting the strength of projection and volume come from the larger supportive muscles. And as the years pass we begin to sound petulant and childish instead of mature and poised.

The voice must never be pushed from the throat. The small muscles there are not strong enough to support such effort and will quickly tire. If you become hoarse after speaking for a half hour or so, check on the diaphragm support you are giving the exhalation which emits the sounds. Place your hand across the front of your throat and if you feel the small muscles at the front and sides tense unduly, return to the breathing exercises suggested earlier. The suggested full deep breath before starting to speak will help relax the throat and place the support where it belongs.

Quality, more difficult to define precisely, can best be described as that characteristic of a tone which distinguishes it from all other tones of the same pitch and intensity. It is sometimes called the timbre, or the German *Klang,* meaning the "ring" of the tone. In describing quality, one frequently uses words that suggest color—a "golden" tone, a "silver-voiced" orator, a "blue" note. It is the distinctive, individual quality of his voice that makes it possible to recognize the friend one hears but does not see.

Quality of tone is perhaps most closely associated with mood and feeling. The connotation, or cluster of associations around the words being read, will help dictate quality. We will discuss connotation more fully in the section on word choice in Chapter Three; for the moment it is enough to be aware that the mood and emotional content of a selection are enhanced by an appropriate vocal quality that underscores the connotation of the words the author has chosen to share a particular experience. Quality, like all the other aspects of vocal and bodily technique, is a part of a whole, and helps the reader in communicating the totality of his selection to his listeners.

Often religious readers unconsciously (it is to be

hoped!) adopt what is commonly called a "ministerial tone." It is pompous and deadly dull. It features an inflection pattern that lifts the end of each minor unit of thought with a rising–drooping–rising double circumflex. This has been referred to occasionally as the "My dear Christian friends" inflection pattern. Just as the listeners pick up cues, whether true or false, about a speaker's sincerity and attitude from posture and gestures, so the "this is the Word of God and it doesn't need any attention from me and you have heard it all before anyway" melody pattern suggests a distancing that can be fatal to vital communication. Alert concentration on what is being said and how it is put together coupled with an honest wish to share the total experience of the literature are the only cures for this occupational disease. If the habit is of long standing the cure will take some time, but it is certainly worth the effort. The Bible consists of literature about people and their relationships with God and one another. It has things to say to us that are moving and important. It presents a wide variety of moods and styles. There is no set, stereotyped way to read it. The reader's vocal and physical techniques must always serve the particular selection.

Rate and Pause

The rate or pace at which a person speaks is often habitual, a part of his personality and his entire background. It probably serves him very well for ordinary conversation, but he may need to adjust that habitual rate to do justice to an author's style and purpose. As with the other elements of vocal technique, the interpreter must train his ear to hear himself in practice and in conversation. There is no magic formula for slowing a too-rapid pace. It requires constant attention. Selecting material with a style and connotation that encourage a slower pace will be helpful. Very frequently the mere physical process of forming a sequence of sounds will affect the rate at which a sentence can be read intelligibly and effectively. Thus, the interpreter will do well to make certain that he is forming every sound accurately and controlling his rate so that this is possible.

Within the overall rate there will be opportunities for subtle and important variety. Emotion, connotation, suggestion, and the combination of vowels and consonants will all provide variation.

Rate includes not only the speed with which sounds are uttered in sequence but also the length and frequency of pauses separating the sound sequences. The beginner is usually afraid to hold a pause long enough for its dramatic effect to register with his listener. If a pause is motivated by real understanding, by identification with the feeling suggested, it may be sustained for a much longer time and with greater effect than the beginner realizes. He need only to be sure that something relevant *to the material* is going on during the pause, first in his own mind and consequently in the minds of his listeners. A pause should usually link what comes before and after rather than break the train of thought progression. When combined with empathy it can be a powerful instrument for emotional implication, but it must always stay within the total concept of the selection and supply whatever transition or suspense is needed.

The interpreter should try not only to use pauses where they will be most effective but also to vary and sustain the lengths of the pauses as the material demands. Punctuation, of course, may serve him as a guide to pauses—but it is only a guide. Punctuation is used on the printed page to signal the eye. It guides the reader in establishing the relationship of words and phrases and their division into sentences. The interpreter can sometimes use changes of pitch or quality or emphasis, or a combination of these, to signal the ear of his listeners. He need not always use a pause. Moreover, it must be remembered that rules and fashions change in punctuation as in everything else. Thus the interpreter's full understanding and response, together with his sense of responsibility to his audience, are the final determinants in the use of pauses.

Intelligibility of Speech

We have already noted that speech, to fulfill its basic function of communication, must be understandable or intelligible, and hence that it must be heard. But to be fully intelligible, speech must be not only audible but also distinct and accurate. The listener cannot keep his attention on the material if he is constantly called upon to "translate" slovenly speech sounds or mispronunciations. Therefore you will want your speech sounds to be distinct and correct as well as pleasing. It is true that nothing is more irritating to the listener than a speaker's self-conscious, overly careful mouthing of vowels and consonants. It smacks of affectation and insincerity and calls attention to the reader and his technique, and away from the material. On the other hand, if the reader cannot be understood he certainly cannot communicate. Consequently, you must strive for habits of pronunciation and articulation that are unobtrusive but sufficiently clear and accurate to enable any audience to understand you.

A distinction between pronunciation and articulation may be helpful. *Pronunciation* assumes that sounds are accurately spoken; it is not immediately concerned with shaping the sounds. *Articulation* refers directly to the shaping of the sounds by the speaker's lips, teeth, tongue, and hard and soft palates. Sometimes it is hard to decide whether a fault is a matter of pronunciation or of articulation. When someone says, "He kep' it" for "He kept it," is the problem faulty pronunciation or slovenly articulation? Probably the listener would decide in this instance that the trouble is, by definition, faulty pronunciation. On the other hand, when he hears a lisping sound, as "thithter Thuthy" for "sister Susy," he wouldn't hesitate in deciding that the difficulty is faulty articulation. Pronunciation is considered acceptable when all the sounds of a word are uttered correctly in their proper order and with accent (stress) on the proper syllable. Current good usage is the guide to correct pronunciation, with a standard dictionary as the final authority.

Biblical names and places can be difficult. Consult a biblical dictionary, encyclopedia or concordance if you are unsure of how to pronounce them. As soon as you are sure of the pronunciation of the word you are going to use, practice it until it comes easily and then say it clearly. Don't pull back and mutter for fear it will get away from you. Your listeners will be distracted both because they didn't really hear it and because of your lack of security with it.

If the reader knows what correct pronunciation is and has checked his own everyday speech, he may profitably turn his attention to improving the formation of sounds and to strengthening their projection. Faulty projection of distinct sounds is closely related to the position of the sound in the word or phrase. The end of the word or phrase is often slighted or left off, even though the preceding sounds are distinct enough. In the exercises for control of sustained exhalation, it was pointed out that adequate control is needed to complete the ends of lines or sentences. This control and the accurate shaping of end sounds are, of course, closely allied. The failure to finish words is one of the faults interfering most with good communication.

The consonant sounds that help most in achieving distinctness are the plosives, *p, b, t, d, k, g.* These sounds are called plosives because the sudden release which completes their formation is a sudden, sharp "explosion" in the air. It is this plosive element that promotes their carrying power. The interpreter should practice common words, alone and in combinations, until he is sure that his sounds, especially the final ones, are distinct. Words like "drop," "cab," "eight," "good," "kick," "gig," "slept," "cribbed," "asked," and "sixths" are examples. Tongue twisters using these and many other sounds are too numerous to mention and are the property of all who know Peter Piper and his ilk. Such jingles are excellent devices for practice in accuracy and flexibility.

The fricative sounds, so called because they escape the speech mechanism with a slight "hiss" of friction (*f, v, s, z,* etc.), also demand particular attention to accuracy in formation. Sometimes, as was suggested in the brief exercise for control of exhalation, the vigor of the escaping sound needs to be toned down. The sounds that give the most trouble in this respect are the everpresent *s* and *z* pair of sibilants. Actually, *s* and *z* are among the most frequently used consonants in the English language. The interpreter should check his articulation carefully when he encounters such lines as

He made the incense altar of acacia wood, a cubit long and a cubit wide—square—and two cubits high; its horns were of one piece with it. He overlaid it with pure gold: its top, its sides . . . . He made two gold rings for it under its molding, on its two walls—on opposite sides—as holders for the poles with which to carry it. . . . He made all the utensils for the altar—the pails, the scrapers, the basins, the flesh hooks and the fire pans: . . . On the north side, a hundred cubits—with their twenty posts and their twenty sockets of copper, the hooks and bands of the posts being silver (Exod. 37:25–38:11, The Torah).

If the sound is too prominent or sharp, a "whistled" s, a slight relaxing of the groove in the tongue, which directs the sound against the teeth, should help. Or perhaps what is needed is a definite shortening or cutting off of the sound by a quicker stoppage of the outgo of air. If the sound of s seems "slushy" or unclear, increased effort should be made to direct the stream of air sharply over the center of the tongue, to expel it centrally between the closely aligned edges of upper and lower teeth. If there is a marked deficiency in the s, or in any other sound for that matter, a speech therapist should be consulted.

This discussion of body control and especially of voice improvement may have seemed unduly detailed to the reader who has not considered the importance of his two-fold instrument for communication or to the one who is already aware of the things we have touched on. To the former let us say you wouldn't try to play the organ to offer a "song unto the Lord" if you couldn't manage the keyboard. For those to whom breathing and voice control are familiar subjects, an occasional reminder of the techniques involved is a guard against developing sloppy habits.

Learning to control the voice and body properly is not arty or theatrical. It is basic in direct and honest communication. The person who feels it is presumptuous to use the best possible technique in reading the Word of God has forgotten perhaps to whom he is indebted for that voice and body.

3

Literary Style

An understanding of the elements of literary style is of prime importance to the interpreter; such knowledge will enrich his comprehension of the material he is reading to a point far beyond the surface meaning. It will give him clues to subtle nuances and relationships that will increase his awareness and consequently enable him to present the selection more completely to his listeners. Awareness of literary style will also help him establish an appropriate pace, use inflections and pauses effectively, and follow the method of organization already present within the selection. The ability to analyze literary style will help the interpreter see how everything works together to achieve a total effect. He will then be able to use his physical and vocal techniques to do the selection the proper service.

The old saying that "style is the man" is of questionable value in the study of biblical literature, since scholars have long disputed the authorship of many of the books of the Bible. Nevertheless, style is a reflection of complex attitudes and environmental influences that have resulted in certain patterns of thought and an habitual vocabulary for expressing those thoughts in writing. It is not enough for the interpreter to accept such phrases as "rhetorical," "majestic," "flowing," "sweeping," or "staccato" as descriptive of the style of a piece of writing. These words describe the way the oral rendition strikes the ear and may or may not be true to the style of the writing. Indeed they may be the result of the reader's imposing his own rhythm and melody pattern on the writing to the extent that there is real distortion. The interpreter must look for clues within the writing—the written style—and use that knowledge to guide him in his use of pace, inflection, pauses, and other techniques of vocal communication.

The elements of literary style which we will consider are:

1. method of organization by which the total idea is developed
2. type, length, and syntactical structure of the sentences within the smaller thought units
3. choice of words and their relationship to one another within particular sentences
4. division of the sentences into speech phrases as they are read aloud
5. rhythm established by the speech phrases as a result of stresses and pauses

In analyzing literary style it is possible to begin at either end of this list or indeed anywhere as long as the selection is finally considered as a total entity with all its parts working in proper balance. As a matter of fact, in the discussions which follow it will become clear that each segment affects and is affected by all the others and that it is impossible to separate these five elements and still produce a total effect that gives the selection its mood, tone, and emotional intensity.

In any close literary analysis of the Bible one is confronted immediately with the problem of multiple translations and editing styles. In the following discussion selections have been made from several texts, followed by brief comparisons between them. The detailed examination of the five elements of literary style is not intended to be evaluatory. It is merely a vehicle for complete communication of what is on the page. It will be the task of the interpreter to look carefully at whatever version he chooses to use and follow a pattern of analysis which will allow him to see how all the elements of style work together to form the whole.

The usual designations for the parts of a public address, i.e., introduction, body, and conclusion, are equally applicable in tracing the pattern of development of thought progression in a piece of literature.

Introduction

If a narrative structure is being used and the unifying principle is chronology, the *introduction* will supply the essential information concerning time, place, characters, and so forth. The New Testament parables often compress this information into a single sentence, as is the case with the account of Jesus' meeting with the centurion in Matthew 8:5–13: "And when Jesus was entered into Capernaum, there came unto him a centurion, beseeching him and saying, Lord, my servant lieth at home sick of the palsy, grievously tormented" (King James). This sentence gives us the time in a sequence of events, the place, the reason for the meeting, the relative social positions of the centurion and his servant, and indicates the centurion's concern for his servant, thus giving us a clue to character and attitude.

Old Testament narratives are more likely to designate historical data of time and place in their introductions. A good example is found in Esther 1:1–3:

> It was in the days of Ahasuerus, the Ahasuerus whose empire stretched from India to Ethiopia and comprised one hundred and twenty-seven provinces. In those days, when King Ahasuerus was sitting on his royal throne in the citadel of Susa, in the third year of his reign, he gave a banquet at his court for all his administrators and ministers, chiefs of the army of Persia and Media, nobles and governors of provinces (The Jerusalem Bible).

It was of course against this background and to notables and important people that Ahasuerus wished to display Queen Vashti in all her beauty and magnificence as his queen. Her refusal to appear then leads directly into the edict which caused Esther's appearance before the King. To ignore the implications and the political importance of such an occasion as the feast is to rob the story of much of its human element as well as its historical significance.

If, on the other hand, the purpose of the writing is to persuade, the introduction will take whatever form has widest appeal to the intended audience. Paul's First Letter to the Corinthians is a masterful use of such an introduction. He first establishes himself and his position in relation to the Corinthians. But he does not depend merely on stating his own position. He stresses his affection for them, his feeling of kinship with them and his pride in their having been converted to followers of Jesus. The entire first chapter is devoted to stressing the need for unity and harmony among them and to the differences between divine wisdom (and folly) and worldly wisdom (and folly). Their wisdom, and even their "folly," is, or should be, divine because of their faith. Thus he has quickly set them apart from the less fortunate and less informed. This implication that one is special is a very effective technique—

much used in modern advertising. The continuing references to affection make the reprimands which follow easier to take. Paul's attitude of humility and service as an agent of Jesus rather than as a leader in his own right gives him an enviable position from which to speak.

Frequently when a writer is primarily concerned with clear and incisive thought or the importance of cause and effect, he uses what we will call "lead-in" sentences to introduce each progressive step in the development, linking each clearly to what has gone before. Paul is also an expert in using this device and can build his case with a lawyer's persuasive logic. Each paragraph picks up an idea, or more often an exact word, from the closing sentence of the preceding paragraph and devotes some time to developing that word or idea, finally linking it clearly and candidly with the next paragraph.

Thus each chapter and indeed each paragraph in 1 Corinthians has its own organization within the greater organization of the whole. More detailed analysis will reveal even more subtle examples of how Paul will elaborate on an idea introduced in a preceding chapter or verse. He will then present an implication, example, or tenet of that idea, move to a conclusion about the idea in its application to all men, and then turn again to "we" or "you" or "you and I." Thus each unit has its own introduction, body, and intimately persuasive conclusion leading neatly into the next major unit which then repeats the pattern. Attention to the attitude established at the beginning of the letter and to the organizational method within the unity of the whole clarifies many seemingly convoluted thoughts.

Within each chapter of the various books of both the New and Old Testament there are "lead-in" sentences which serve to focus the attention of the reader or listeners and prepare them for what follows. The interpreter must take care to use them for precisely the same purpose.

The tradition of fragmenting chapters and books into small sections of a few verses each has lead in part to a regrettable loss of organization and sometimes to a misrepresentation of basic attitude. If you were not using the entire letter to the Corinthians, for instance, which admittedly would be practical only under certain circumstances, it is important to remember the tone of the introduction in relation to the entire selection and let its influence be felt. Failure to do so in this case could have reduced Paul's affectionate but firm reprimand and his fatherly advice to a near harangue.

Body

After the introductory unit has accomplished its purpose, the writer moves into the *body* of his material, that is, into "the heart of the matter." This is frequently done by amplifying a thread or detail or concept set forth in the introduction by presenting examples or by taking a more detailed look at various aspects of it or by developing it into a larger issue.

In a narrative the body begins when the plot and action, for which the introduction has given us the time, place, and characters, begin to develop. In non-narrative prose the movement into the body of the writing is usually very easy to discern. In the Epistle to the Romans, for example, the address and thanksgiving and prayer serve as the introduction; the introduction concludes with the statement of the theme Paul will follow and the quotation from the Old Testament, "The upright man finds life through faith" (1:16–17, The Jerusalem Bible). He then moves directly into the various aspects of that theme, or "the heart of the matter."

In the brief and relatively unfamiliar letter of Jude,

which has no chapter divisions, he wastes no time after his greeting in getting to his purpose with "I have been forced to write to you now and appeal to you to fight hard for the faith" (verse 3, The Jerusalem Bible). He then mentions the people who are threatening the faithful and, in order that there be no mistake, he adds "I should like to remind you," then "Next let me remind you;" and "remember, my friends." Thus the steps in organization are clearly defined as he leads them and us from one major thought unit into the next.

Conclusion

The third major unit in organization is the *conclusion,* which pulls together the main threads of the introduction and the high points of the writing contained in the body of the material. The conclusion may take one of many forms; it may be a summary, a deductive or inductive reasoning pointing to a philosophical tenet, a call for action, or a significant question growing out of the examination of various factors, to mention only a few. The conclusions to the Epistles are clearly set off and usually return to the tones set in the greeting. Often there is a formal summation in the form of a doxology as well as the final greetings and blessings. In the biblical narratives, the conclusion is usually brief and simply tells us of the action that followed as a result of the climax or that the characters left the scene and went to another place.

The Book of Esther has, in effect, two conclusions. The first completes the story of the Jews' peril and revenge and Esther's part in the ultimate outcome. The conclusion of the Book itself establishes the resultant dates of the Feast of Purim and in some versions authenticates the story itself as well as the Greek translation made by Lysimachus.

Thus there is an overall organization of introduction, body, and conclusion, and often, especially in the Bible, this organization operates within the chapters or smaller units as well. It is important to remember that those ideas grouped together in a paragraph, or in a stanza of poetry, work in very close relationship to each other and form a cluster of associated minor thought units. The division into chapters in the Bible is based on this unity of incident in the narratives and of precept in the non-narrative units. It is helpful in analyzing the entire thought progression to pay attention to ideas that are clustered together and also to the contribution each cluster makes to the total progression.

Sentences

The second element of literary style concerns the structure of sentences, which are, of course, units of thought within the larger units of paragraphs or biblical chapters. The interpreter will find the relative length of the sentences in a selection a most interesting contributing factor to overall style, and when reading aloud an awareness of the grammatical complexities will serve as an important guide to him in controlling pace, using pauses, and creating areas of emphasis, as well as establishing the general tone of communication between writer and reader or listeners.

Although there are numerous classifications of sentences according to type, we will be concerned only with the simpler designations such as declarative, interrogative, imperative, and exclamatory, and, as we move into syntax, a brief look at complex and compound construction and suspended and attenuated sentences.

In actual practice we as listeners tend to suspend our attention through a sentence until we know by traditional clues of inflection and pause that the reader or the speaker has completed the thought with all its modifications and inserted qualifications. Thus the sentence as a unit is important to the interpreter who is trying to infuse the symbols on the printed page with meaning and relevance for his listeners.

A simple declarative sentence moves in the expected order from "who" or "what" to the action. Since with this type of sentence our minds need not hold an idea in suspension while waiting for qualifying phrases and clauses, there is a satisfying sense of completion. The sentence is usually brief and conclusive. Thus when it is inserted among longer, more complex sentences, it provides us with an interval in which to gather our thoughts about previous statements or focus clearly on a new idea.

This technique of juxtaposing simple and complex sentences is effectively used in the opening chapter of Genesis, which we will examine in detail later in this chapter.

Questions, or interrogative sentences as they are formally called, may be either direct or rhetorical. The direct question will be followed by an answer and is usually found in dialogue and in drama. A rhetorical question is used to introduce a topic or underscore a point, and no answer is expected. Sometimes the question itself is unanswerable or the answer is already well known and therefore need not be articulated. Paul makes use of many such questions in 1 Corinthians to force his audience into the proper response. Many of them are lead-in sentences.

An interesting use of the interrogative is to be found in Job 38, where God poses a long series of questions. God starts many of his questions to Job with "Can you?" or

"Did you?" or "Have you?" By their direct interrogation and the use of "you" they seem to demand an answer, which in Job's case can only be negative. As the speech progresses the questions become more rhetorical and serve as lead-in sentences for descriptive passages in the declarative form in which God demonstrates his power and wisdom. The combination of interrogative and declarative lends an interesting variety to the section and sets up a rhythm of focus that shifts from Job, to whom the questions are addressed, to God, who controls all the elements and wild creatures over which Job is powerless. An interrogative sentence implies a pause to enable the listeners to formulate at least a mental answer and will therefore have an effect on pace.

An imperative sentence cuts directly into the minds of the hearers since it is a command for some action on their part. Sometimes the command is directed rather toward some other agent whose action will directly affect the listeners, as in the first chapter of Genesis which is an excellent example of the effective use of varying types of grammatical structure. Notice how the direct statement "God said" introduces each new episode; what God said is then expressed in the imperative form: "Let." The sentences involving the actions of creation become more complex in structure with qualifying clauses and phrases as the days progress, but each action is concluded with the simple direct statement "And so it was," or a variation of this wording. Moreover, each day is concluded with an identical declarative sentence.

Exclamations often cause the interpreter some discomfort. The appearance of the exclamation point seems to us moderns to indicate some special, emotionally charged break in the continuity of thought. However the exclamation point, like most punctuation, is simply an eye signal. It contributes to the sense of the preceding word or words, and since exclamations are frequently not complete sentences, it serves to identify them as interjections within the complete thought. They usually do indicate a heightened emotion but they are quite simple to handle if you look upon them as a contribution to, or commentary on, what has immediately preceded or, more frequently, is about to follow rather than as important in themselves. Exclamation points were quite fashionable in previous centuries when some of the translations were made, just as dashes and semicolons seem to be in vogue at the present time. Let the sense and emotional level dictate whether the exclamation should stand as a high point by itself or whether, as is more usual, the interjection should be blended into the following statement.

The word order of sentences is also important. Whatever is given us first in a sentence we tend to put foremost in our minds. When the opening word or words serve to connect two related ideas or events as in "on the other hand" or "at a later time," we respond by holding the previous thought suspended in our attention until the counterpart has been completed. The opening sentence of Genesis has this suspending effect whether the translator has chosen to say, "In the beginning," as is true of most Christian versions, or "When God began," with which the modern Torah opens. In all versions, a particularly telling shift in word order comes at the climax of God's work with only very slight variations on the following:

God created man in the image of Himself,
in the image of God He created him; (created He him)
male and female He created them. (created He them)

Sentence Length

Obviously the length of a sentence tells us very little in itself, but it is affected by the complexity of thought being expressed and, in turn, affects the rhythm and flow of thought as well as the division into speech phrases and the amount of stress needed for clarity. Thus a rhythm of thought and a rhythm of sound flow are established when long, syntactically complex sentences alternate with or are interspersed by short direct sentences.

In the following discussion we will be designating sentence length by numbering syllables within each sentence. It would be ridiculous to assume that you must count every syllable of every sentence in the Old and New Testaments before you can communicate the Bible to your listeners. The numbering of syllables is simply a way of graphically representing sentence length as we look at the relationship between its parts. It is usually enough to note relative length or brevity, although for the serious scholar of literary style it is also interesting to observe the subtle patterns that develop within a well-written selection.

Let us look at the syllable count per sentence in three versions of Genesis 1. We will quote from King James, The Torah and The Jerusalem Bible translations and then take a look at the variations in style.

Genesis 1 (King James)

In the beginning God created the heaven and the earth.

And the earth was without form, and void; and darkness was upon the face of the deep. And the Spirit of God moved upon the face of the waters.

And God said, Let there be light: and there was light.

And God saw the light, that it was good: and God divided the light from the darkness.

And God called the light Day, and the darkness he called Night. And the evening and the morning were the first day.

And God said, Let there be a firmament in the midst of the waters, and let it divide the waters from the waters.

And God made the firmament, and divided the waters which were under the firmament from the waters which were above the firmament: and it was so.

And God called the firmament Heaven. And the evening and the morning were the second day.

And God said, Let the waters under the heaven be gathered unto one place, and let the dry land appear: and it was so.

And God called the dry land Earth; and the gathering together of the waters called he Seas: and God saw that it was good.

And God said, Let the earth bring forth grass, the herb yielding seed, and the fruit tree yielding fruit after his kind, whose seed is in itself, upon the earth: and it was so.

And the earth brought forth grass, and herb yielding seed after his kind, and the tree yielding fruit, whose seed was in itself, after his kind: and God saw that it was good.

And the evening and the morning were the third day.

And God said, Let there be lights in the firmament of the heaven to divide the day from the night; and let them be for signs, and for seasons, and for days, and years:

And let them be for lights in the firmament of the heaven to give light upon the earth: and it was so.

And God made two great lights; the greater light to rule the day, and the lesser light to rule the night: he made the stars also.

And God set them in the firmament of the heaven to give light upon the earth,

And to rule over the day and over the night, and to

divide the light from the darkness: and God saw that it was good.

And the evening and the morning were the fourth day.

And God said, Let the waters bring forth abundantly the moving creatures that hath life, and fowl that may fly above the earth in the open firmament of heaven.

And God created great whales, and every living creature that moveth, which the waters brought forth abundantly, after their kind, and every winged fowl after his kind: and God saw that it was good.

And God blessed them, saying, Be fruitful, and multiply, and fill the waters in the seas, and let fowl multiply in the earth.

And the evening and the morning were the fifth day.

And God said, Let the earth bring forth the living creature after his kind, cattle, and creeping thing, and beast of the earth after his kind: and it was so.

And God made the beast of the earth after his kind, and cattle after their kind, and every thing that creepeth upon the earth after his kind: and God saw that it was good.

And God said, Let us make man in our image, after our likeness: and let them have dominion over the fish of the sea, and over the fowl of the air, and over the cattle, and over all the earth, and over every creeping thing that creepeth upon the earth.

So God created man in his own image, in the image of God created he him; male and female created he them.

And God blessed them, and God said unto them, Be fruitful, and multiply, and replenish the earth, and subdue it: and have dominion over the fish of the sea, and over the fowl of the air, and over every living thing that moveth upon the earth.

And God said, Behold, I have given you every herb bearing seed, which is upon the face of all the earth, and every tree, in which is the fruit of a tree yielding seed; to you it shall be for meat.

And to every beast of the earth, and to every fowl of

the air, and to every thing that creepeth upon the earth, wherein there is life, I have given every green herb for meat: and it was so.

And God saw every thing that he had made, and, behold, it was very good. And the evening and the morning were the sixth day.

Genesis 1 (The Torah)

When God began to create the heaven and the earth—the earth being unformed and void, with darkness over the surface of the deep and a wind from God sweeping over the water—God said, "Let there be light"; and there was light. God saw that the light was good, and God separated the light from the darkness. God called the light Day, and the darkness He called Night. And there was evening and there was morning, a first day.

God said, "Let there be an expanse in the midst of the water, that it may separate water from water." God made the expanse, and it separated the water which was below the expanse from the water which was above the expanse. And it was so. God called the expanse Sky. And there was evening and there was morning, a second day.

God said, "Let the water below the sky be gathered into one area, that the dry land may appear." And it was so. God called the dry land Earth, and the gathering of the waters He called Seas. And God saw that this was good. And God said, "Let the earth sprout vegetation: seed-bearing plants, fruit trees of every kind on earth that bear fruit with the seed in it." And it was so. The earth brought forth vegetation: seed-bearing plants of every kind, and trees of every kind bearing fruit with the seed in it. And God saw that this was good. And there was evening and there was morning, a third day.

God said, "Let there be lights in the expanse of the sky to separate day from night; they shall serve as signs for the set times—the days and the years; and they shall serve as lights in the expanse of the sky to shine upon the earth." And it was so. God made the two great lights, the greater light to dominate the day and the lesser light to dominate the night, and the stars. And God set them in the expanse of the sky to shine upon the earth, to dominate the day and the night, and to separate light from darkness. And God saw that this was good. And there was evening and there was morning, a fourth day.

God said, "Let the waters bring forth swarms of living creatures, and birds that fly above the earth across the expanse of the sky." God created the great sea monsters, and all the living creatures of every kind that creep, which the water brought forth in swarms; and all the winged birds of every kind. And God saw that this was good. God blessed them, saying, "Be fertile and increase, fill the waters in the seas, and let the birds increase on the earth." And there was evening and there was morning, a fifth day.

God said, "Let the earth bring forth every kind of living creature: cattle, creeping things, and wild beasts of every kind." And it was so. God made wild beasts of every kind and cattle of every kind, and all kinds of creeping things of the earth. And God saw that this was good. And God said, "Let us make man in our image, after our likeness. They shall rule the fish of the sea, the birds of the sky, the cattle, the whole earth, and all the creeping things that creep on earth." And God created man in His image, in the image of God He created him; male and female He created them. God blessed them and God said to them, "Be fertile and increase, fill the earth and master it; and rule the fish of the sea, the birds of the sky, and all the living things that creep on earth."

God said, "See, I give you every seed-bearing plant that is upon the earth, and every tree that has seed-bearing fruit; all shall be yours for food. And to all the animals on land, to all the birds of the sky, and to everything that creeps on earth, in which there is the breath of life, [I give] all the green plants for food."

And it was so. And God saw all that He had made, and found it very good. And there was evening and there was morning, the sixth day.

Genesis 1 (The Jerusalem Bible)

In the begining God created the heavens and the earth. Now the earth was a formless void, there was darkness over the deep, and God's spirit hovered over the water.

God said, 'Let there be light,' and there was light. God saw that light was good, and God divided light from darkness. God called the light 'day,' and the darkness he called 'night.' Evening came and morning came: the first day.

God said, 'Let there be a vault in the waters to divide the waters in two.' And so it was. God made the vault, and it divided the waters above the vault from the waters under the vault. God called the vault 'heaven.' Evening came and morning came: the second day.

God said, 'Let the waters under heaven come together into a single mass, and let dry land appear.' And so it was. God called the dry land 'earth' and the mass of waters 'seas,' and God saw that it was good.

God said, 'Let the earth produce vegetation: seed-bearing plants, and fruit trees bearing fruit with their seed inside, on the earth.' And so it was. The earth produced vegetation: plants bearing seed in their several kinds, and trees bearing fruit with their seed inside in their several kinds. God saw that it was good. Evening came and morning came: the third day.

God said, 'Let there be lights in the vault of heaven to divide day from night, and let them indicate festivals, days and years. Let them be lights in the vault of heaven to shine on the earth.' And so it was. God made the two great lights: the greater light to govern the day, the smaller light to govern the night, and the stars. God set them in the vault of heaven to shine on the earth, to govern the day and the night and to divide light from darkness. God saw that it was good. Evening came and morning came: the fourth day.

God said, 'Let the waters teem with living creatures, and let birds fly above the earth within the vault of heaven.' And so it was. God created great sea-serpents and every kind of living creature with which the waters teem, and every kind of winged creature. God saw that it was good. God blessed them, saying, 'Be fruitful, multiply, and fill the waters of the seas; and let the birds multiply upon the earth.' Evening came and the morning came: the fifth day.

God said, 'Let the earth produce every kind of living creature: cattle, reptiles, and every kind of wild beast.' And so it was. God made every kind of wild beast, every kind of cattle, and every kind of land reptile. God saw that it was good.

God said, 'Let us make man in our own image, in the likeness of ourselves, and let them be masters of the fish of the sea, the birds of heaven, the cattle, all the wild beasts and all the reptiles that crawl upon the earth.'

> God created man in the image of himself,
> in the image of God he created him,
> male and female he created them.

God blessed them, saying to them, 'Be fruitful, multiply, fill the earth and conquer it. Be masters of the fish of the sea, the birds of heaven and all living animals on the earth.' God said, 'See, I give you all the seed-bearing plants that are upon the whole earth, and all the trees with seed-bearing fruit; this shall be your food. To all wild beasts, all birds of heaven and all living reptiles on the earth I give all the foliage of plants for food.' And so it was. God saw all he had made, and indeed it was very good. Evening came and morning came: the sixth day.

To graphically represent the variations as simply as

possible we have charted the sentence lengths by indicating the number of syllables each one contains, we have grouped the sentences by day divisions.

	King James	The Torah	The Jerusalem Bible
First Day	10–17–12–11–17–12–10	54–19–12–13	15–27–10–15–12–10
Second Day	23–25–6–11	16–32–4–6–14	19–4–24–6–11
Third Day	25–24–34–33–10	26–4–17–7–32–4–32–7–13	25–4–20–29–4–33–6–10
Fourth Day	56–26–41–10	53–4–30–35–7–13	30–15–4–27–30–6–10
Fifth Day	29–34–23–10	30–41–7–27–13–29	27–4–31–6–30–10
Sixth Day	30–34–50–22–46–41–39–15–10	29–4–27–7–16–30–43–37–42–4–14–13	26–4–22–6–53–32–20–25–33–29–4–14–10

The King James version of this first chapter of Genesis has thirty-three sentences varying in length from six to fifty-six syllables. The repeated sentence enumerating the days has just ten syllables except for the sentence pertaining to the second day, which has eleven. There is no clearly discernible predominance of sentence length but in general length increases as the acts of creation progress, and the three longest are those dealing with the creation of the lights in the firmament, the creation of man and God's blessing on man. The longest sentence deals with the sun, moon, and stars and concludes the creation of inanimate things.

The 1967 version of The Torah, on the other hand, has forty-two sentences, and though they range from four to fifty-four syllables, more than half of the sentences are under twenty syllables long. In all of the units after the opening four sentences we find effective use of an alternating between long and short sentences. Notice particularly the pattern in the description of the third day. In the first sentence of the third day unit (verses 9–13), God separates the water from the dry land. This completed, we are told "And so it was." This is followed by the naming of the earth and the seas, followed by "And God saw that this was good." In the next sentence God creates the vegetation. When that is finished, we have "And so it was." In the next sentence the vegetation comes forth, and again the next sentence tells us "And God saw that this was good." The paragraph closes with the enumeration of the day. The arrangement and progression are clearly and sharply logical.

The length of the sentences reflects this organization, with the patterns of 26, 4, 17, 7, 32, 4, 32, 7, 13. Thus our minds are carried through a relatively long sentence in which God expresses his next idea, and then halted for the simple four-syllable statement of the actualization of that idea, "And so it was." This is followed by a longer sentence perfectly balanced into two parallel clauses which name the two parts. Then we read a shorter, seven-syllable statement of God's pleasure and satisfaction in the accomplishment.

We are again suspended through the thirty-two-syllable sentence in the unit that tells of the more complex decision to create the vegetation. This is followed again by the four-syllable sentence of its actualization. Immediately there is another long sentence telling of the appearance of the vegetation, which is followed by the short seven-syllable expression of God's satisfaction. The unit closes with the relatively brief statement of the completion of the day, which follows, of course, the established pattern of parallel clauses. This pattern of alternating between long and short sentences is repeated fairly consistenly throughout the account and sets up a rhythm of suspension and steadying which can be very helpful in clarifying the organization and progression of events and their significant relationship to one another and to the total act of creation.

The creation as recounted in The Jerusalem Bible, contains forty-five sentences ranging in length from four to fifty-three syllables. Again the technique of alternating between long and short sentences is used up to the creation of man, with that section being treated in two of the longest sentences in the chapter. In addition, the predominance of medium-length sentences of between twenty-five and thirty syllables makes the fifty-three syllable sentence found in the section on the creation of man stand out in contrast.

Thus the King James version, in part because of its continuing use of "and," gives a sweeping and cumulative quality to the creation with the result that one is caught up in the vastness of the whole accomplishment. The Torah and The Jerusalem Bible distinguish more clearly between each step of the creation, and the divine order and interdependence of all created things seem more apparent.

This very brief and fragmentary look at sentence lengths as they relate to organization and rhythm is not intended to imply that you must count every syllable of every sentence before you read from the Bible. It merely serves to point out a means of using an attribute already present in each of the translations and versions, for enriching and clarifying the relationships between the various parts of a large unit of biblical literature.

Syntax of Sentences

Inseparable from a consideration of sentence length is a discussion of the contribution of syntax to style. Obviously the more clauses and phrases within a sentence, the longer it must be to accommodate them. The extremely short sentence, to be a sentence at all, is necessarily confined to a simple syntactical structure.

We are so accustomed to syntax as a sort of formula for the relationship of words to one another that we often assume that our listeners will immediately straighten out any complexities which exist in our speaking. Usually this is true, but the interpreter must be careful not to distort word relationships by false pauses or misleading inflection and emphases. It might be well to remind ourselves of the simple rules we learned so many years ago. Nouns and pronouns are the names of objects, places, or people. Verbs carry action or state of being. Adverbs limit or qualify those actions or states of being. Adjectives describe or qualify the objects or places or people for which nouns stand. Phrases and clauses are means of further qualification or expansion. The heart of every sentence, no matter how complex, is the subject, which is a noun or pronoun, the verb, which gives it its action, and the object of that action. Thus in the opening complex sentence quoted earlier from the Book of Esther, the core of the sentence's structure is, "It was in the days of Ahasuerus," and all the rest of the words expand or qualify this statement. The second sentence depends upon "he gave a banquet." The core ideas must emerge clearly to provide a springboard for the rest of the sentence.

Any discussion of syntactical elements in biblical literature brings one, of course, to the highly important principle of parallelism. Although parallelism is basic in

Hebrew poetry, it is also an important rhythmic characteristic of biblical prose. Parallelism ranges from the simple
repetition of identical phrases such as "And so it was," to
the more complex correspondence in sense and balance
in form between successive lines of a unit. We shall delay
a more detailed look at parallelism until we reach the
discussion of poetry, where it is basic to the rhythm. The
emphasis of parallelism as instrumental in achieving
thought return and consistency of sentence length, however, must not be underestimated even in the prose sections of the bible.

Parallelism can become a very real stumbling block to
the reader who does not handle it carefully. There is danger
of its being monotonous and repetitious, or worse, a
rhythmic drone which we have heard before and therefore makes us drowsy and unresponsive. The classic example is probably Paul's discussion of love in 1 Corinthians.
Many a wedding ceremony has been marred by a poor
reading of this essentially beautiful passage. The reader
must be aware that Paul's use of parallelism is basically
a balancing of the positive and negative aspects of response
to one's fellow man. Realization of the need to keep the
balancing, with a slight emphasis on the qualities which
love *is*, will help make the passage meaningful.

Parallelism may also be used in the expansion or condensation of an established idea. It can be used most effectively for this purpose, but the mind of the reader must
remain constantly alert for the danger that it may become
a mere listing. Each new step, especially in an elongated
parallelism such as we find in 1 Corinthians, must set up
a quality against which another unit will be weighed.

The simple diagram of the first paragraph of Genesis
on page 69, taken again from The Torah, will graphically
elaborate on the above discussion of syntax. It indicates
the complexity of the first sentence, which does not reach

Diagram of Genesis 1:1–5

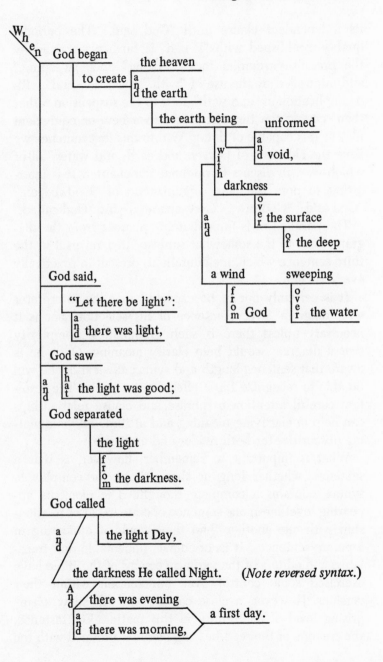

its independent clause until "God said." The periodic quality established with "When" is further sustained by the present participial forms, "being" and "sweeping," and intensified by the use of "with." Even the "and" with its implication of "and with" adds to the suspension rather than moving the thought ahead to a new or equivalent idea as it is capable of doing. Within this first sentence we have the elements of heaven and earth and water, all of which we will discuss throughout the chapter. It is interesting to note the clear organization of "God began," "God said," "God saw," "God separated" and "God called."

The parallelism is immediately apparent from the diagram, even to the somewhat sophisticated reversal in the third sentence which, incidentally, is present in practically every version.

It is certainly not to be expected that the interpreter will "diagram" every sentence of his selection, nor is it necessary unless there is such grammatical complexity that a diagram would help clarify meaning. Once he is aware that sentence length and syntax affect style, he will be able to recognize those effects quite easily. The resultant careful attention to phrase and clause relationships can help in clarifying meaning and attitude and eliminating obscurities for both reader and audience.

What is important to remember, however, is that a sentence, whether long or short, simple or complex in syntax, contains a complete thought. The elements appearing together in one sentence operate in closer relationship with one another than they would if appearing in separate sentences. It is, of course, undeniable that translators and editors of the various versions of the Bible have exercised some control over punctuation within their versions. However, a close comparison will show a surprising level of conformity in this matter. For instance, the creation of the seed-bearing plants is grouped with the creation of the trees that bear their seed within their fruit, since these two are species of the same general category. The same is true of the creation of the birds, the fish, the creeping creatures, and the cattle. Male and female, as the two divisions within the creation of man, are kept within the same thought unit and thus, in Genesis 1, are simultaneous in their emergence, both partaking of the image of God.

A reminder of our earlier warning about the interpreter's dependence on punctuation is perhaps wise here. Punctuation is intended to signal the eye to, for example, group related phrases and clauses or separate a series of descriptive adjectives. Terminal punctuation marks, periods, question marks, and exclamation points, indicate visually the tone of the thought unit as well as its termination. Colons and semicolons indicate a balancing of units within a sentence. Commas separate and group minor thought divisions. A comma, despite what some of us were taught somewhere between kindergarten and college, does not always mean a pause. The interpreter can often handle a list of qualifying adjectives without a pause between each word. Dashes of course indicate an interrupted or suspended thought as do parentheses. Punctuation, it must be remembered, is for the eye and is not an infallible guide to the use of pause or inflection.

Word Choice

A writer or speaker chooses his words first of all for their denotation or dictionary meaning. A combination of letters producing a word immediately calls to mind the object or attitude or action or concept which that word symbolizes, whether we see it written or hear it translated into a combination of sounds. But there are many synonyms for even most of our common words, and one word is chosen over another for its shade of meaning. There is, for example, a difference between a puddle, a pool, a lake, and an ocean. There is a difference between weep and cry, and keen and moan and wail and bewail and bemoan. The differences lie in the *connotation* or cluster of associations which has grown up around each word and will have an important effect on the empathic response of both reader and listeners.

Some of the factors contributing to the connotation of a word are personal and subjective on the part of the reader or hearer, but in general they have a universal source. A writer, too, will have subjective associations for certain words that render them most useful for him in specific contexts, but he must choose words with a compatible universal connotation as well so that his audience will grasp the associational context without being misled from his desired meaning.

A really skilled writer will test his words for harmony of sound as well. Certainly literature written from the oral tradition, as was most of the Bible, will bear strong aural influence. This of course is the special province of the interpreter. It was once fashionable to contend that certain sounds gave certain effects to the words in which they were used, such as the *s*, the liquid *l*, and the voiceless *p* in sleep. This contention is only partially true. Certain combinations of sounds, because of the difficulty or ease with which they are articulated, flow more smoothly than others. However, there is a greater difference between the way we say "sleep" and "slip" and "slap" and "slop" than the mere shift of vowel sound. The difference lies partly in articulation but primarily in connotation.

The words used in the Bible are predominantly simple in both denotation and connotation. Difficulties sometimes arise for the modern audience with respect to archaic place references, allusions, and metaphors, but the basic diction is simple. This is especially true of the Gospels in the New Testament where simple men are reporting Jesus' words and actions as he moved among people of all classes. It is a mistake, however, to ignore subtle differences within the various versions. Look, for instance, at the same phrase as it appears in the three different versions of Genesis 1. "The Spirit of God moved upon the face of the waters" (King James), "a wind from God sweeping over the water" (The Torah), and "God's spirit hovered over the water" (The Jerusalem Bible). Basically they all *mean* the same things. Try reading the three examples aloud, being careful to form the sounds fully and correctly and to be aware of the connotations involved in the verb forms; you will find three different tones being suggested by "moved upon," "sweeping over," and "hovered over."

We will refer again to the sound and connotation of words when we discuss poetry in a later chapter, but it is important to be aware of the contribution of vowel combinations and consonants even in prose.

The contribution of sound to meaning is referred to as *tone color* and it embraces onomatopoeia, alliteration, assonance, and consonance. Certainly one does not break up one's reading into separate vowels and consonants. But some attention to clear articulation and proper pronunciation as well as to the connotation of the word as a unit will be profitable in establishing mood and in clarifying progression of thought.

Closely allied to choice of individual words is the use of figures of speech such as metaphors, similes, and personifications. The Bible is particularly rich in these literary devices. Similes and metaphors, and by extension personification, are all methods of appealing to our senses in order to compare one thing to another. A thing or person looks or sounds or acts like some other object or person whose qualities are sufficiently well known to us that we easily make the transfer from one to the other. In choosing the analogies a writer is interested in a synthesis of qualities, of course, but there is usually one outstanding characteristic such as strength, gentleness, richness of taste, odor or texture, size, or characteristic activity which embodies the second member of the comparison but that is not always so characteristic of the first. The comparison is effected through appeals to the senses and depends for its effectiveness, as we pointed out in Chapter Two, on the reader's or listeners' willingness to respond to what they see, hear, smell, touch, taste, and feel, both tactually and thermally, as well as to the muscle tension and relaxation accompanying the sense appeals.

The Bible is so full of similes and metaphors that it would be impossible to attempt to list them all outside of a concordance, where indeed there are several pages of references under "like" and "as." In handling these figures of speech and in making full use of personification as well, the interpreter must rely on empathy and voice quality for help in describing the suggested attributes without losing sight of the first part of the comparison. Most biblical figures of speech are brief and placed in a context where this control is no problem. Complications arise when the comparisons are packed very closely together and contain somewhat different attributes, as is often the case in Song of Songs, Psalms and the visions in the prophetic writings. In these instances, the original object, such as "my beloved," controls the unity, and the things to which the beloved is compared provide the variety which shows the many facets of the beloved.

The Old Testament is filled with similes using fire, most often devouring or blinding in its brillance and intensity. Water is sometimes a roaring sea, sometimes "rain on mown grass," sometimes a flowing river; it is also used in numerous other forms which suggest qualities of power, refreshment, continuance, and so forth. Trees and seeds and grass are also favorite figures, sometimes growing and flourishing and again withering for lack of water or care or from an act of God, and becoming chaff which is useless and blown away by the winds. Birds are sometimes gentle doves but may often be pelicans and ostriches lost in a wilderness. Animals are perhaps the most prevalent objects of comparison. Many of them are wild and terrifying, such as lions, beasts of the wilderness, and even dragons. On the other hand, there are the lambs and sheep which were so familiar to the shepherds and wandering tribes and which even today carry a strong implication of helplessness and docility.

The objects used to draw comparison in the New Testament are most often allusions to crops, harvest, plows, sowers, boats, fish, nets, and simple household articles. There are more doves than pelicans and more lambs than lions. This, of course, is completely in harmony with the content, especially of the Gospels and Acts, where the accounts are most often of gentleness and love.

Some of the most interesting comparisons in both Testaments, but especially in the Old Testament, are those which imply a type of action and utilize primarily kinetic and kinesthetic imagery. The strength of Samson is depicted through his actions, of course, and one of the most telling similes is the description of his breaking the ropes from his arms "like threads." The Psalms have a wealth of action similes including "runneth after me like a giant," "ready to burst like new bottles," "feet like hinds' feet," "skip like a calf," "spreading himself like a green bay tree," "hills melted like wax," "stretched out the heavens like a curtain," and many, many others. "The mountains skipped like rams" and "the little hills like lambs" is a particularly delightful and carefully wrought pair of comparisons. The actions implied must be reinforced by muscle tension or relaxation, not only for the actions themselves but for the effect such actions had on the observers.

Some of the comparisons are strange to modern audiences, and the interpreter will need to understand the second term of the comparison whether or not he explains it to his hearers. A reference to a spearhead like a weaver's beam, for example, may be misunderstood or meaningless unless we remember that "beam" in this sense is a large heavy roller on which fabric is wound during the process of weaving. A spearhead of that size and weight would be an awesome thing! Voice and muscle tone must suggest this awe.

Before leaving the figures of comparison, we cannot resist mentioning one or two which are perhaps less familiar than some but which seem even to the modern reader peculiarly apt. One is the description in Judges 7:12 which tells us that the "Midian and Amalek and all the sons of the East stretched through the valley as thick as locusts; their camels were innumerable like the sand on the seashore" (The Jerusalem Bible). Anyone who has ever seen a field in which a swarm of grasshoppers has settled can immediately picture the vast crowd. The discrepancy in size between human beings and locusts and camels and grains of sand makes the number even larger. This is the reverse of the technique used in Revelation 9:7 where locusts are compared to horses. One last simile out of Proverbs, which of course is made up almost entirely of such figures of speech, cannot but bring up a strong response: "Confidence in an unfaithful man in time of trouble is like a broken tooth and a foot out of joint" (25:19, King James).

Probably the most important point which can be made about word choice in the Bible is to remind ourselves that those who spoke or wrote these words were living, vital people. Their speech was alive and they were avid listeners. Their words reflect their daily lives and, in the Old Testament particularly, their overwhelming concern with Yahweh's approbation or condemnation. Their praises were shouted or sung in "new songs." Their pleas were for their freedom and the fate of their nation. Their rebellions and arguments were strongly motivated. Their history was their salvation. In the New Testament Jesus' gentle power and even his righteous anger were alive and vivid. His apostles were often afraid or awed or filled with simple doubt and confusion. The crowds which followed him were real people with real concerns, and Jesus spoke to them in words chosen to comfort, or clarify, or instruct them according to their abilities to respond. Too often the words of both Testaments become merely "words in the Bible." They are, even for us today, words of life and all its daily struggles. They must be kept as alive for communicator and receivers as they were when they were first chosen. They must be used to share very human experiences.

Speech Phrases

The last two elements of literary style, the division of sentences into speech phrases and the rhythm of stresses and of flow of sounds resulting from this division, are not always mentioned in a discussion of written language. However, they are of considerable interest to the interpreter because they become evident only when the literature is read aloud.

Syntax, as we have already remarked, is in reality a set of rules and customs which clarifies the relationships existing within sentences. Consequently, in a long sentence or one where special emphasis is required on one section or another, a speaker will probably set off the units with pauses of varying lengths, thus grouping the words for easy comprehension of their relationship. In this way the sentence is broken into what we call speech phrases.

Again the most practical way to graphically represent this discussion is to indicate length of speech phrases by the number of syllables each contains although one reads by words and phrases, not by syllables. Incidentally it can be very helpful to take a close look at the way in which one habitually breaks the sentences in the Bible. Custom may have established in our minds a pattern that is robbing the passage of its living quality. Or perhaps we are imposing our own rhythm on the writing and the result is monotonous or too broken to carry the appropriate tone. An occasional check on how we are actually reading a familiar excerpt may be very revealing.

The interpreter will allow punctuation to guide him in the establishment of his speech phrases, but he must remember that he cannot and need not translate all of these visible clues into pauses of equal length and importance; change of inflection and quality of voice are often equally effective. The way in which a sentence is divided into speech phrases will be dictated by the need for emphasis, clarification of relationships, and all the other factors we have discussed. Two interpreters might vary in their decisions on speech phrase divisions but there are numerous guidelines available in the writing which should not be ignored. It is, of course, not necessary that there be perfect unanimity.

For example, when a concept is established it is important to make its component parts quite clear. When it is referred to again and again, as is the case in parallelism, it is usually not necessary to set off the parts with such precision after the first repetition. At the close of each unit of the creation in The Jerusalem Bible, to return to an example we have used before, the enumeration of the day just completed is expressed in these words: "Evening came and morning came" followed by the indication of the number of the day. The first time this is used, the interpreter would probably divide the sentence thus: "Evening came / and morning came: / the first day." This division into units of 3–4–3 syllables establishes the progression from evening to morning and emphasizes the fact that this was the first day of all and that the period is designated as a "day." To place such divisions on the successive numerations of the days would become monotonous and quite unnecessary. We now expect morning to follow evening and the designation of number to follow in sequence. The fact that that division of time is designated as "a day" is also familiar to us. Thus we would probably read it: "Evening came and morning came: / the second (third, etc.) day," and the division into speech phrases would become 7–3 (7–4 in the case of the second day since "second" has two syllables).

Similarly, the King James version would probably read 4–4–3–1: "And the evening / and the morning / were the first / day," changing it to a smooth phrase of twelve syllables for successive days. We are here considering "evening" as a two-syllable word as it is pronounced in acceptable modern diction. The Torah, which reads "And there was evening and there was morning, a first day," using balancing independent clauses for evening and morning, would be most comprehensible and true to textual style if the division were 5–5–2–1 the first time "day" is mentioned, and then remained 5–5–3 (or 5–5–4 in the case of "second day") throughout the chapter.

Prose Rhythm

Although we are accustomed to thinking that rhythm is an attribute of poetry, a close examination will show that prose has a rhythmic base too. Admittedly it is not as regular and perceptible as that found in poetry but it is nevertheless present. We have already suggested that the sound flow of speech phrases of comparable length can become a factor in rhythm.

Within each speech phrase there are certain stresses, some of which are required for pronunciation and others of which are rhetorical, that is, required for clarity, emphasis, and relative importance. Speakers differ in their speech rhythm and this helps contribute to their oral style. The interpreter, however, must adapt his rhythm to what he finds on the printed page. There will always be some differences among interpreters in the use of pauses and stresses, but by careful analysis an inherent rhythmic base can be found. Parallelisms, as mentioned earlier, will affect stresses as ideas are repeated and expanded.

Continuing with the consideration of Genesis 1, it is interesting to note that in the King James version, although sentence lengths contribute little to a significant pattern except in their repetition, there is a preponderance of speech phrases of four syllables each and numerous examples of seven-syllable phrases. The pattern begins to emerge, in the opening paragraph, as outlined below. The speech phrases are divided by slashes, and the stresses are marked in the usual manner where they are necessary for pronunciation or for emphasis and clarity. The heavier stresses will clearly vary in degree, but the division into speech phrases will help to differentiate between lighter and heavier stresses.

1 In the beginning / God created the heaven / and the earth.
2 And the earth was without form, / and void; / and darkness / was upon the face of the deep.
3 And the Spirit of God moved / upon the face of the waters.

4 And Gód sáid / Lét there be líght: / and there wás
líght.

5 And Gód sáw the líght, / that ít was góod: / and
Gód divíded the líght / from the dárkness.

6 And Gód called the líght / Dáy, / and the dárkness
he cálled / Níght.

7 And the évening / and the mórning / were the fírst
/ dáy.

Within the first seven sentences, then, we find:

Sentence	Syllables per Speech Phrase	Stresses per Speech Phrase
1	5–7–3	2–3–1
2	7–2–3–8	3–1–1–3
3	7–8	3–3
4	3–4–4	2–2–2
5	5–4–7–4	3–2–3–1
6	5–1–6–1	3–1–2–1
7	4–4–3	1–1–1

Indeed part of the pleasure in the King James version of the Bible comes from the highly rhythmic pattern of speech phrases of comparable length and the arrangement of the stresses within them. This same patterning, incidentally, has also been the downfall of the inattentive reader who allows himself to be so swayed by the melody of some passages that they no longer carry any meaning. The "ministerial tone" with its rising inflection on the second or third word of every phrase and its final circumflex inflection is an almost inevitable result of this lack of balance of attention between what is being said and how it is being said.

Much of the criticism of the newer translations stems from a change from the familiar rhythm. However, a careful look at speech phrases and stresses within those speech phrases will reveal that each version does have a rhythmic base of its own. It is worse than futile to try to carry over the rhythmic elements of one translation into another. The Jerusalem Bible, for instance, has a very marked pattern of stress linkage from one paragraph to the next in Genesis 1. The two-stress speech phrase opens and closes almost every paragraph. Within the paragraphs there is variety, but only fourteen sentences out of the forty-five are completely lacking in two-stress speech phrases.

Rhythm, then, as it is established in length of speech phrases and the presence of stresses within those speech phrases, can be a very important tool for the interpreter in establishing mood and heightening emotional appeal. It must be remembered, on the other hand, that rhythm must never be sought for its own sake when we interpret the Bible. It must underlie and support the content. To give it too much prominence is as bad an error as to fight against its presence. The *how* must never obscure the *what* of the literature you are communicating.

Literary style, then, is the sum of many elements working together to produce a total effect. It is the material with which the interpreter must work. Too often it is ignored in reading the Bible aloud because we have been accustomed for centuries to listening only for the message contained in the writing. It is indisputable that the message is clearer when supported by full use of the style in which it is expressed. A simple paraphrase can give us the gist of any chapter or verse. Only careful attention to how the content is organized and expressed can give us the Word of God with all its inspiration and emotional relevance in a time when we are bombarded by the most skillfully persuasive writing and speaking the world has ever known. We live in a constant turmoil of words being brought to us with the express purpose of persuading us to action. The Bible is certainly worthy of at least as much analysis, concern, and appreciation.

4
Narratives

It is both impractical and unnecessary for the interpreter to attempt a sharply categorical classification of the various sections of the Old and New Testaments according to literary form. Some books, such as Genesis, Exodus, Samuel, and Chronicles are primarily classified as history while other accounts, such as the stories of David and Elias, and the Book of Kings fall more comfortably into the category of biography. However, both history and biography are basically narrative in their literary form. Moreover, if judged by their purpose, which scholars agree is informational in both cases, they share a clear distinction from fiction and myth, which are primarily imaginative. They closely resemble folklore in that they are often based on fact but treated imaginatively.

Obviously, there are subtle differences which make these categories no more than practical working classifications, and the interpreter will need to pay careful attention to the variations within each particular selection.

We shall look at the characteristics of narrative writing in general and at the demands that these characteristics make upon the interpreter, and then turn our attention briefly to some of the differences between Old Testament and New Testament narratives.

A narrative tells a story. It tells what happened to whom and usually where and when, and sometimes how and why. A narrative may be true or fictional or a combination of both. Our concern here is not with establishing the factual or mythical basis of the units we will be considering but rather with looking at how the authors, whoever they may be, chose to handle the elements of what happened to whom, where, when, how, and why.

As we have said, most of the narratives in the Bible have many of the characteristics of folklore. They were often orally transmitted, and the sounds of the words and the rhythmic elements frequently resemble the literary qualities of poetry. Memory and imagination are freely blended. There are sometimes quite different versions of the same story with numerous apparent discrepancies. The contrasting versions of the great flood come immediately to mind as do the differing accounts of the creation, the fall of Adam and Eve, and the birth of Jesus, his Passion and death. The facts of birth and death are present in all versions but the amount of detail varies widely.

Folklore, passed from storyteller to storyteller, always exhibits these discrepancies. What appeals to one storyteller and his audience will be elaborated and extended while other elements of the story are minimized since they may not contribute to its imaginative and emotional appeal. Folklore often reflects local or national characteristics, resulting in changes of emphasis in the details used to illuminate the story line from one version to another.

Biblical narratives, especially in the Old Testament, are compact and swift moving. The language is concrete and appeals directly to the senses. Feelings are expressed rather than described or discussed. Restraint of anger, joy, or grief was not a virtue in the primitive life from which folklore springs nor were speculation and philosophical discussion favorite occupations.

The subject matter is clear and the plot line moves rapidly and without detour through the incident being related. The organization is largely chronological and any relevant past information is usually given directly and briefly as the story opens; the outcome of the story is not often delayed by elaborate devices of suspense. The characters are sharply contrasted with one another. They offer types rather than complex three-dimensional characterizations. We are given succinct descriptions such as a comment on age, or physical strength, or beauty, but seldom any details regarding individual features, appearance, or attitude.

The oral tradition assumes a strong sense of directness and an acute awareness of audience response on the part of the storyteller. It is at this point that the modern interpreter of biblical narratives encounters his first problem. The stories are already so familiar to him and to his hearers that he is tempted to ignore the importance of his role as storyteller. He just reads the words and neglects to share the experience of the story with his hearers. The important words here are *share* the *experience* of the *story*.

In order to share an experience we must relive it actively ourselves. We must become involved in what happened to whom in order to involve our listeners. This requires total control and response of voice and body and above all the active concentration of an informed and responsive mind.

We touched on the importance of focus and projection in our discussion of the use of the voice in interpretation. We also discussed muscle tone and empathy in the use of the body. All of these elements are a part of the important principle of directness. However, directness is first of all a mental matter. The interpreter thinks *to* his audience. He receives the stimulus from the printed page, having already prepared the selection so thoroughly that he knows how every part fits into the whole. He reacts to it mentally and sparks vocal and physical responses within himself. He then turns his attention *out to* his audience, using his vocal and physical techniques to reach their minds and emotions. He does not make them come to him. He goes to them.

This may seem to be a difficult concept in theory. But we all know the feeling of attempting to recount some humorous or serious incident by which we were so moved that we were eager for our listeners to know every detail so they might experience the same emotion. We concentrate on making the chain of events as vivid as possible. Our bodies and voices reflect the tensions or relaxations which colored the experience for us. We almost unconsciously use every technique to hold their attention as we suggest places, the people involved, the steps leading to the climax, and the impact of the climax itself. Too many readers of biblical and religious literature surround themselves with a mist of theological footnotes with the result that the stories are never brought to life. The more familiar the story, the more effort it requires to make it vivid enough to achieve its full purpose. A truly good reading may provide a listener with his first *real* experiencing of what the story says. Remember that the narrative form is probably as old as man and has always been popular because it re-creates an experience so vividly that the listeners may share in it.

A narrative always has a narrator who selects and arranges details for their effect upon the audience. The interpreter takes his cue from the narrator and becomes himself the re-creator of the experience.

Point of View

One element peculiar to narration which grows directly out of the presence of a narrator is *point of view*. Point of view is the physical and psychological position that the narrator takes in relation to the action, the characters, and the resultant plot. The narrator is the mouthpiece used by the author. The degree of characterization which the author gives him may range all the way from the first person narrator who is himself involved as a character in the plot to an almost totally detached third person narrator who simply reports what he sees and hears. Between these two extremes there are innumerable variations.

A narrator, whether he is speaking in his own person as "I" or in the third person, may be omniscient, knowing what everyone is thinking and telling of events which he could not possibly have witnessed within the framework of the story. On the other hand, he may exercise this omniscience in regard to only one or perhaps two of the characters. He may have a distinct personality of his own or he may simply be a "someone" telling the story. He may comment on events or characters or he may let them speak for themselves.

Point of view is sometimes called "perspective" or, as Henry James prefers to describe it, "a central intelligence" which selects details and makes implications that give the story its own peculiar touch. It is of extreme importance to the interpreter both in his analysis of a selection and in his performance. The same series of events told by different people with different degrees of involvement will vary considerably, as Robert Browning so skillfully shows in his famous account of a murder trial in *The Ring and the Book*. Although the terms *point of view, perspective,* and *central intelligence* are modern in their application to narration and often applied chiefly to prose fiction, the concept is highly useful to anyone reading biblical literature.

At first glance it would seem that most of the narrators in both the Old and New Testaments are objective third person storytellers. On closer examination, however, we find a wide variety of viewpoints. The narrator in the Book of Kings, for example, moves in and out of the story, sometimes letting an episode complete itself and then moving in for a specific comment on either the event or the character involved or both. The narrator in the story of Joseph is sometimes almost obliterated by the quick succession of events and by his skill in keeping our attention focused on Joseph and his family. Nevertheless, he tells us secret thoughts and fears and ambitions in the minds of the characters and is even omniscient in his knowledge of Yahweh's care and commendation of Joseph through his career.

The parables of the New Testament offer a particularly interesting study of point of view. Without becoming involved in an examination of authorship, it is quite clear that one event, such as the agony in the garden or the birth of Jesus, or the resurrection, can be chronicled with strikingly different effects by different writers. Although Matthew, Mark, Luke, and John are all strongly sympathetic to Jesus, we need only compare such episodes as the Sermon on the Mount as told by Matthew and as told by Luke to be aware that the purpose of the retelling, the memory of what was important, and the evaluation of details all differ sharply. John, too, often turned the narrative to serve the doctrinal points he wished to make. This is not to say that their recorded memories are to be disparaged but rather that a narrative always depends on who is speaking and out of what environment.

Action and Plot

The *action* of a narrative is the sequence of visible or discernible happenings. The *plot* is a sequence of changes in human relationships which runs parallel to the action and is occasioned by and manifested in the action.

The action in biblical narratives is the basis for their organization. It is, of course, closely related to the progression of time and place, which we will discuss later. It must be remembered that the Hebrews saw life in terms of conduct, that is, actions, rather than in terms of thought as did the Greeks. What a man did brought God's immediately apparent approval or God's rebuke and punishment.

There is a great deal of physical activity in the biblical narratives although it is never elaborately described. It is indeed often stated as starkly as "His brothers went to pasture their father's flock at Shechem," followed within three sentences by "He [his father] sent him from the valley of Hebron and Joseph arrived at Shechem" (Gen. 37:12–15, The Jerusalem Bible). Nor is this starkness of action detail limited to the Old Testament. The parables are almost universally characterized by the tremendous condensation of activity, as for example, "Immediately afterwards the Spirit drove him out into the wilderness and he remained there for forty days, and was tempted by Satan. He was with the wild beasts, and the angels looked after him" (Mark 2:12–13, The Jerusalem Bible). These two sentences conclude the extremely brief account of Jesus' baptism, the climax of which, of course, is in verse 10, where we are told that the heavens opened and the Spirit descended on him. The interpreter must use these introductory or transitional or conclusive statements effectively in order to preserve that organization of action essential to the plot.

Climax

A *climax* is the peak moment in a series of events. There can be a *climax of action,* which is sometimes called the *crisis* and after which the events can go in only one direction. It is built up to by an accumulation of key events which must be emphasized to the listeners. There is also a *climax of plot,* or a high point in the development of human relationships. Frequently, the climax of action and the climax of plot occur together or in close sequence. Some narratives have what might be termed a climax of single character development as their main thrust. This is the point at which the character reaches his highest point of development, the point toward which the plot and action have been moving him. In extended narratives, such as the story of Joseph or the account of the trial and crucifixion, each step in the overall organization has its own major or minor climax and they occur in rapid succession.

A climax of whatever kind always implies a building up of tension and intensity. Sometimes the tension is very slight but it is always present. In biblical literature as well, the climaxes carry tension, but all too often familiarity with the narrative tempts the interpreter to assume that this increase of tension will emerge without his help. If the plot, often the essential comment on humanity's relationship with God, is to carry impact, the interpreter must allow his bodily response to help him. The discussions of empathy and muscle tone in Chapter Two are particularly applicable here.

In almost every biblical narrative the narrator reports

the climax of action and frequently the climax of plot as well. In the parable of the Prodigal Son, for instance (Luke 15:11–32), it is the narrator who tells us of the return of the son, and we must identify with the father's joy at seeing him from afar in order that the welcome and celebration will ring true. The reader must visualize the arrival and let his body and voice express the motivation for the father's greeting speech. As always, empathy and muscle tone are of great importance. One must look carefully for the clues to be found in kinetic and kinesthetic imagery and respond to them.

Time and Place

We have said that a narrative tells what happens to whom and sometimes where, when, why, and how. The "where" and "when" that the action takes place may or may not be important. Modern narratives often use a very sophisticated and complex method of telling the reader, and hence the interpreter and his audience, what they need to know about time and place. There is the flashback technique, for instance, in which significant information is inserted after the plot and action have begun in the present. In biblical stories, however, time progression almost always takes the form of a simple chronology within individual episodes. Part of the reason for this, perhaps, is the ancient Hebrews' linear concept of history, especially the history of the race and its inseparable religious history. Part of the reason may be the fact that these stories almost certainly came from the oral tradition of the storyteller whose chief purpose for retelling a familiar tale was to remind his listeners of the implications and results of the action rather than to present a full and novel setting. In any case, the sequence of time is basic to the organization of what happened first, then next, and then finally. This progression must be clear to the listeners so that the experience of the incident or incidents has a beginning, a high point, and a conclusion.

Often the elements of time and place operate on at least two planes in biblical literature. In the prophetic writings, for instance, the narrative units are often drawn from the past history of Israel, are reexperienced by the prophet in the very recent past, and frequently carry a promise for the future. However, the actual telling is immediate and done in terms of a present problem and audience. The entire Acts of the Apostles is a report of past action as it was seen and heard by Luke. He gives us the time and place transitions, identifies the apostles involved, and then records the event or speech. The speeches are put into direct discourse as if they were verbatim, which may or may not be true. Nevertheless, the fact that the speaker is acting directly gives them immediacy, and the frequent references to the past and to prophecies which have been fulfilled are inserted in the light of present developments.

Although place names are often used without any description, the names themselves frequently convey geographical characteristics of the area. But it is the genius or spirit of the place which was important to the Hebrew mind; historical significance, of the nation as it developed or within the narrator's or character's own lineage, was more important than the outward features of the place. Thus strong associations have significance because they pertain to a particular locality.

There is a basic difference between being at home and being in a foreign country, especially if you are in exile. There is a difference between a seashore and a desert and between a crowded, busy city and a path in an olive grove. There is a difference between a hilltop where the countryside is visible for a great distance and an enclosed, fertile, protected valley. These differences are further underscored by the dependence which the biblical characters felt upon nature for food and clothing as well as shelter. Seasons of planting and harvest are often important clues to the details of setting. The interpreter will find that his knowledge of history will sharpen his awareness of the effect which various locations have on both action and plot.

Houses and dwellings are not often described beyond an indication of the wealth or position of the owner, which is implied in his occupation. The only full description of a building in the Old Testament is that of the temple built by Solomon in Jerusalem, and even then the fact that it is located in Jerusalem is of primary importance. Whenever a description is given or even an adjective used, it must receive careful attention. This is equally true of possessive pronouns. When a man goes down into *his own* house or a tribe comes to *its own* land, there is an accompanying feeling of peace and security which is essential to the plot.

Journeys are important in the Bible, and the kinetic and kinesthetic imagery resulting from them grows out of the previously mentioned sense of the spirit of a place, as a beginning or an end point. There was dread and sorrow and a great weariness in the journey into exile but different feelings about the journey out of exile.

Characters

We have said that the basis for organization within most biblical narratives is the action. The action may involve Yahweh's appearing at the moment of climax and speaking directly to the others involved in the story, or the earthly creatures themselves or, not infrequently, the elements or some object such as a stone or a burning bush or a dividing sea acting on the command of Yahweh. The *plot*, however, involves changes in human relationships, either with other human beings or with Yahweh. Thus we come to a consideration of character.

Most of the information we need about the characters in biblical literature is given directly by the narrator. Sometimes, as in the case of Reuben who intended to save Joseph from his brothers and return him to his father, the narrator tells us what is in the character's mind as he completes a certain action. More frequently, however, the actions speak for themselves.

We learn about a character in a piece of literature by noting what he says about himself and what others, including the narrator, say about him. He also reveals himself in his actions and his responses to the actions of others. There are numerous instances of this throughout both Testaments. We said earlier in this chapter that the characters in many biblical writings are typical rather than complex. Nevertheless, there are some like Jonah who show strong traits of individuality. Even those who are typical have attitudes and responses that underscore their essential strength or kingliness or holiness or weakness.

The most important aspect of a biblical character is his inner response pattern, which grows out of his attitudes toward himself and others, toward his environment, and toward actions performed by himself and by others. These dictate his responses and his consequent actions. His exterior qualities, such as age, sex, position in society, physical health, and so forth, strongly influence his inner qualities, that is, his attitude toward himself and others, his sense of values, and thus his degree of psychological and emotional tension in a given set of circumstances. He is complete only when the interior and exterior qualities are logically related.

In order to become involved in the action and plot of a story, the listeners must be aware of what kind of person is speaking or acting. It is not enough to depend totally upon the narrator's descriptions because there are often sections of direct discourse and even some indirect discourse that reflect the inner qualities of the character. The interpreter must use his voice and body to suggest the state of mind, in its broadest sense, of the character himself. When the narrator creates a scene and peoples it with characters who speak or whose thoughts he knows and reveals, the interpreter must reflect all he is given of the characters' responses.

This is not to say that the interpreter of biblical literature becomes an actor and stages a scene. But neither is he simply a reporter. Empathy, muscle tone, and posture do much to suggest strength or fear or great sorrow or joy. These emotions are likewise reflected in pace, rhythm, and general tone of vocal communication. One can often detect the emotional key of a conversation even when the words are not discernible. You cannot expect an audience to believe the words they are hearing if you, the communicator of those words, look and sound detached and unmoved and uninterested. You must *share* the *experience with* them.

A thorough analysis of all the inner qualities of a character and the use of physical and vocal techniques to project those inner qualities and their exterior manifestations are extremely important factors in the interpretation of biblical literature; the listeners may be already familiar with the action but may not have yet shared in the implications of the changes in human relationships which form the plot and thus carry the true impact of the narrative.

· The Bible is so full of narratives that it is difficult to find very much material which does not partake of some of its characteristics. Stories have always had an enormous appeal. They are extremely effective devices for illustrating and clarifying whatever may lie slightly beyond the grasp of finite minds. We can understand by analogy and parable what we cannot comprehend in any other way because the telling is vivid and allows us to relate in a personal, experiential way. Consequently, when the reader attempts to underplay the story elements in a narrative selection with the hope of making it more relevant for a modern audience, he is, in fact, defeating his own purpose. The stories charmed us as children, and when they are properly re-created, they hold our interest and bring us new insight as adults. Their very familiarity helps establish a sense of continuity which modern man so desperately needs.

5

Narratives in
the Old Testament

The Old Testament's demands on the oral reader are great. Aside from the fact that it contains examples of almost every type of literature, there is a complexity of references and a wide variety of style. It is common to divide the writings of the Old Testament into the classical (or pre-exilic) period and the romantic (or post-exilic) period. This generalization is useful for categorizing, but it is important to remember that the lines between these periods are not at all distinct and, as within any other "movements" in literature, changes occurred slowly and with considerable overlapping of characteristics.

It is more helpful to the interpreter to examine a selection from the standpoint of its individual organization and literary style, the techniques of narrative writing that it exhibits, and the details and variations requiring his attention. This must be done, of course, against the awareness that the Old Testament is basically a history of a nation and that the story form is used as a means of historic emphasis.

There are three types of history, all of which are found

throughout the Bible. Some history is descriptive and tells of what took place. There is a didactic history which points out a lesson, as does much of Kings 2, for example. And there is the more sophisticated "scientific" history which emphasizes cause and effect and tends to overlap the other two types. The first type is less concerned with "message" than the second and third. Thus the purpose of the story and the intended receivers will influence the narrator in his choice of style, characters, and method of organization. These are the important clues for the interpreter. Since much of the history is in fact biography, particular attention must be paid to the aspects of character analysis, which we have already discussed, in order that the man being used as a symbol may emerge with all his strength or holiness or anger or power. Sometimes there is more heroism than pure history, as is possible in the Book of Daniel; but that, too, often had its purpose, in this case encouraging the people at the beginning of a long and difficult period of war and conflict.

Characters

The characters of the Old Testament narratives reveal themselves in their speeches, sometimes directly and sometimes through the narrator who reports not only what they said but also the motivation behind the speech. They also, of course, reveal themselves through their actions, which the narrator reports concretely and vividly, usually without comment on motivation beyond our general assumptions based on situation and general temperament or position. But it must be remembered that many of the characters' decisions and consequent actions grew out of the associative power of the linear concept of the past and a limitless concept of the future in Yahweh's presence. The strong are tremendous, and the weak, the cunning, the wicked, the wise, and the good are equally pure in type. Nevertheless, by their very explicitness they provide considerable insight into human nature and must not be treated as caricatures. Gestures and speeches are realistic. When a king wishes someone summoned into his presence he says so. When he punishes a slave, we are told of it without elaboration or rationalization.

Because of their purity of type, most of the characters in the Old Testament will not give the interpreter much trouble as he considers their attributes. The modern reader may need to remind himself of some aspects of ancient law and the importance of family and lineage to fully understand the motivations for their actions. However, they usually fulfill exactly the requirements of their particular positions in life.

But there is another and more difficult problem of characterization in the handling of the voice of God in the Old Testament, just as there is in the direct discourse attributed to Jesus in the New Testament.

We do not know how God sounded when he spoke. We do not know how he looked, indeed he usually was not seen at all as a person. But we do know the Hebrew and Christian concept of his power and strength and of his constant concern for the good or evil of the actions of mankind. In the opening chapters of Genesis, for instance, God is going about a tremendous task with authority and efficiency. He uses the imperative "Let" with the complete assurance that it will immediately be done. There is majesty without aggressiveness. The interpreter must give the account the dimension it requires. When each episode is completed, the satisfaction and approval must be made evident.

On the other hand, when God spoke to Samuel (Sam.

1:3), he explained his future action to the boy with carefully controlled reasonableness, veiling his anger against
the House of Eli. His anger was not veiled, however,
when he delivered his curse on Satan (Gen. 3:00), and
this attitude must certainly be suggested in the interpreter's body and voice. His attitude toward the opinion-
ated and self-righteous Jonah is one of tolerance that approaches humor, and his position of wisdom as he speaks
to Job is partly revealed by the fact that he leaves much
unsaid that Job would wish to hear. God's speeches are
full of devastatingly reasonable questions to which Job
can give only one answer. A close look at word choice and
overall rhythm will be helpful in discovering and communicating the attitudes of both speakers.

Analysis and projection of character are also interesting
and important in those sections of the Bible which are
essentially short stories, such as the Books of Ruth, Jonah,
and Esther. For instance, in Esther it is important to be
aware that the incident is made relevant and acceptable
because of the kind of person involved and the particular
customs of the era. Notice the relatively small amount of
dialogue during the first part of the story. There are many
things which need to be explained to us, such as those
mentioned in our brief discussion of the introduction to
the Book in Chapter Three. The narrator takes us through
an extended period of time rich with Persian manners and
customs until Esther is established as Queen. Only then
do we encounter much dialogue, as she pleads with Ahasuerus. The proclamations, of course, are put into direct
discourse, but it is not until Haman has his ill-fated inter-
view with the King that the dialogue again emerges as
conversation. The narrator controls the story and presents
the characters "in scene" as it were, wherever there is a
one-to-one conversation.

The Book of Ruth has been called a story without a

villain. It is an idyll of love and domestic happiness. Therefore the characters are drawn with more depth of human response than those we find in Esther. It exhibits perfect unity of their development and the growth of their relationship despite the fact that the narrator does not stop to analyze them for us. There is no need. The motives are clear and perfectly understandable within the context of the customs and laws by which they lived. In our discussion of time and place we mentioned the importance of one's own land and people. This consideration is certainly at the heart of the story of Ruth and adds strong, vivid undertones of loneliness and courage as she follows the harvesters to glean the grain. The writing style is simple and yet moves with a serene dignity due in part to the balanced sentences frequently connected by "and." They are relatively long and have an easy, flowing rhythm.

There is an abundance of dialogue which allows the characters to reveal their thoughts and attitudes more clearly than if the narrator simply reported what they said or thought. Care must be taken that their attitudes toward one another are strongly suggested when the material is read aloud. The action develops because of the kind of relationship they have with one another; otherwise, it becomes only a sentimental tale with a happy ending. We must believe in these people and in their gentle tolerance and devotion. They speak directly and intimately to each other, and the interpreter must make his listeners aware of this as he reads.

Jonah, of course, provides one of the several examples of humor in the Old Testament. Human like the rest of us, he shrinks from the call he is given and tries to outwit God. God plays his game with him and Jonah loses every hand! It is not meant to be authentic history but is a satire in the form of an allegory. There are such delightful touches as "They [the sailors] already knew that he was trying to escape from the Lord, for he had told them so" (1:10–11, The New English Bible), and when we remember that he had not told them his business or his country or nation, we are amused at the picture of Jonah confiding his plight to a group of rough seamen. Later, after Jonah's repentance from inside the fish, we find, "Then the Lord spoke to the fish and it spewed Jonah out on dry land" (2:10, The New English Bible). There is a delightful playfulness in the great and mighty God speaking with the fish about this matter.

And finally there is the picture of Jonah, pouting and angry, sitting (with his arms crossed, one is sure) outside the city, while the mighty God who caused a turmoil in the sea causes a vine to grow to shade him and then takes it away to teach him a lesson which could have been done with one mighty stroke. Except that God understands and tolerates the Jonahs among us.

Setting

The Hebrew storyteller was brief and omitted elaboration of setting, as we mentioned earlier. The stories were presented directly and with immediacy. Two factors probably contributed to this brevity and directness, the first being the fact that almost no members of his audience could read and the impact had to be made sharply since the oral tradition is purely temporal; the audience could not stop and rework a part which was not clear on first hearing. Also, Hebrew syntax lent itself particularly well to this condensation. For one thing, there were very few dependent clauses to qualify or ornament the telling. Very rarely was clause subordinated to clause. Perhaps more important was the peculiar quality of the verb tenses.

Tense

Studies of the ancient Hebraic language have revealed no clear-cut sequence of tenses. There seems to have been no verb form like our past participle depending upon "have." The past was the simple past tense. However, when a narrator spoke of a past action he often conceived of it as the present. That is to say, he took himself and his listeners back to the event rather than bringing the event up into the light of the present. This, of course, stems in part from the concept of permanence deeply rooted in their tradition of the typical and universal, and in their continuing active awareness of Yahweh whose laws remained unchanging. Nuances of past tense such as the imperfect and the participal forms were sophisticated later additions to most languages.

Many scholars believe that there were only two tenses for the verbs. One tense set forth a *continuing* action whether it was past, present, or future, while the other tense was used for completed action which might be past, present, or future. Thus the immediacy of action would be heightened. In any case, the modern reader must be careful that transitions of time and place, for instance, are not slighted and that each factor of character description is fully used. The stories are often paragraphed for changes of character or scene rather than for purely logical breaks or groupings in thought content to which we referred in the chapter on style.

Climax of Plot and Action

The brevity and immediacy of which we have spoken have an effect on the speed and impact of climaxes whether they are minor ones within episodes or the major climax of an extended story. It is extremely difficult to pinpoint the major climax of plot in such an extended and complex narrative as the story of Joseph because of the careful interweaving of elements of family history and of various people who operated in close relationship to Joseph. It has been a great convenience to ritual but a great disservice to the Old Testament as literature that we have come to think of the Bible as a series of separate short episodes rather than a series of continuing, interestingly structured units. In the interest of practicality it is useful to talk about each episode as a literary unit, but it must be remembered that, for example, as the story of Joseph unfolds the protagonist grows in strength and maturity and as we are frequently reminded, Yahweh was with him, and Yahweh made everything he undertook successful.

Joseph greeting his brothers in chapter 42 is quite a different person from the young boy who enquired politely for information about them in chapter 37, verses 16 and 17, and he is again reacting differently when he greets his father in a later chapter. The authority which has been given him must be evident in his bearing and tone in chapter 42, while his deep devotion to his father as well as his position to act in his behalf will affect his thinking and thus his posture and pace of speaking in chapter 46.

Recalling the Hebrew concept of a God who showed his approval or anger in this world, rather than storing up man's good and evil deeds in this world for reckoning in the next, it becomes evident that the intervention of Yahweh is really the essential unifying force of the total narrative, with the actions of Joseph and the subplots and changes in human relationships resulting from this main motivation. Thus the *climax of action* is probably Joseph's final "promotion" to Governor of Egypt. Each episode has its minor climax of action, however, as he succeeds in each endeavor.

It is interesting to note, also, that after this point in Joseph's achievements another plot line, which began with Joseph's dream and which is concerned with Joseph's relationship to his family, takes prominence. Thus the *climax of plot* as it concerns Yahweh's relationship to Joseph is probably his interpretation of the dream for which God had given him the knowledge. The climax of the relationship between Joseph and his family is the ultimate test (chapter 44), and the brothers' resultant actions give to Joseph the answer he has been seeking throughout the years about their relationship. This new relationship is fully revealed and solidified in chapter 50. Again each episode touching on the family has its own minor climax of plot. Character development parallels the dual plot development.

Narrative Style

There is almost a perfect proportion between dialogue and narration in the story of Jonah. It is interesting to contrast God's choice of words and the simplicity of syntax used when he speaks to Jonah with some of the utterances he makes in the more crucial and historic situations. His charge to Jonah is simple and direct: "Go to the great city of Nineveh, go now and denounce it, for its wickedness stares me in the face" (1:2, The New English Bible). One need only compare this command with the call given to Moses, for example, to realize that here is no solemn, momentous mission that will shape the history of a mighty people.

The story of Noah and the flood has some very interesting elements for the interpreter to examine. Scholars agree that any version is a composite narrative, which may account in part for some of the contradictions from one to another and certainly must have some bearing on the diversity of style within any single translation. This diversity of style is, of course, important to the interpreter, who must make full use of the variety without losing the unity of the sequence of events.

The actual story of the flood begins in Genesis 6:5. It is difficult to say exactly where it ends since God's covenant to man is such an important conclusion. Even the introduction is more complex than many of the sections of the Old Testament, despite its compactness and brevity. Verses 5 through 7 give us God's sorrow at man's wickedness and God's regret of his magnificent act of creation. This will require careful handling because it conveys a balance of sorrow and annoyance which must motivate all the rest of the action. Verse 8 gives us Noah. But we are not told at that particular point why he had "found favour with Yahweh," although within the context it is evident that he was still a righteous and good man and must therefore be spared. The first mention of Noah is followed by the statement that this is his story. We are then told of his goodness and his three sons, Shem, Ham, and Japheth, but in the very next two sentences our attention is turned again to the earth's corruption. Thus within twelve verses we have God's motivation, Noah's qualifications for survival, and are introduced to his sons who will figure prominently in sequences which follow the covenant and the flood.

We then move into a sort of extended introduction to the actual flood with God's explanation to Noah of his intention. There are specific instructions for the building of the ark and the promise of a covenant. This is a great deal of diversified material to crowd into four verses; God continues his building instructions, and we are told that Noah did all that God ordered him to do. Next come the specific instructions about the animals and birds, and again Noah does all that Yahweh orders. Then there is a disconcerting interruption in the chronological progress with the statement of Noah's age, which is in itself startling. His age itself is perhaps less important to the interpreter than the second half of the sentence, "when the flood of waters appeared on the earth" (7:6, The Jerusalem Bible). Because we have already been prepared that there will be a flood, there is danger that the information of its arrival may be lost. It is important that it be emphasized that the flood waters have indeed come and the flood has begun.

After Noah has everyone on board, we are told, "And Yahweh closed the door behind Noah" (7:16, The Jerusalem Bible), or, "Then Yahweh shut him in" (The Anchor Bible, vol. 1), or, "and the Lord closed the door on him" (The New English Bible). It is interesting that all three of these modern versions use similar concluding statements to bring the preparation unit to an unmistakable conclusion. Now we and Noah and all those aboard the ark are ready for the journey.

It is at this point that we encounter one of the most startling shifts in style. Verses 17 through 24 are rich in parallelisms. They give us a graphic description of the rising water with

> The waters swelled, lifting the ark until it was raised above the earth. The waters rose and swelled greatly on the earth, and the ark sailed on the waters. The waters rose more and more on the earth so that all the highest mountains under the whole of heaven were submerged. The waters rose fifteen cubits higher, submerging the mountains (The Jerusalem Bible).

This powerful scene brings us to the climax of this section, in which everything is destroyed. The destruction is repeated in three successive sentences using the verbs "perished," "died," and "destroyed," and "only Noah was left of the story which begins with the mention that it was and those with him in the ark." The technique is almost cinematic as we watch the water rising and see the ark sail away, then observe a long shot of the mountains as they disappear, finally focusing back on the ark.

This unit opens with a mention of the forty days of flood which God had said he would send, but it ends confusingly with a statement that the water rose for one-hundred and fifty days. It can, of course, be assumed that the rain continued for forty days and the water continued to rise even after that, if one is inclined to be unduly concerned about this discrepancy. The references to a specific length of time, however, do serve to bracket the description and can certainly be used to indicate a great passage of time no matter how the days were reckoned.

After the ordeal of the flood our attention is immediately returned to God's relationship with Noah and the occupants of the ark. Gradually the waters begin to subside. We are even given the exact day of the month when the ark came to rest on the mountains of Ararat. And nearly three months later, on the first day of the tenth month, the mountain peaks which were the last to disappear become visible. The precise time sequence in the rest of the account can be very helpful in ordering the events until that moment when Noah can look out and see that at long last the surface of the ground is dry! And we know that vegetation has already begun to grow again because the dove has brought back a new olive branch. And again we are given the exact day of the exact month and Noah's precise age. Thus the flood is over and the cycles of nature are beginning again.

The story itself ends here (Gen. 8:14) with historical precision but it is usual to include in the telling the account of God's new covenant which continues through 9:17.

The unit on the covenant begins with God's greeting to

Noah. As he had closed the door at the beginning of the journey, he now tells Noah to disembark with all his household and animals and birds. Noah immediately offers sacrifice on a newly built altar, and Yahweh is pleased with him. Then follows the promise, which God makes first to himself and which all modern versions put into poetic form. Then there is the blessing and the clarification of the covenant between God and "every living thing that is found on the earth" (Gen. 9:17, The Jerusalem Bible).

The organization and progression is much simpler in the covenant unit than in the description of the preparation for and duration of the flood. The changes in style are less abrupt and more consistent with the character of Yahweh, who is the only speaker. The narrator, too, returns to a more usual style. Thus, the only problem inherent in this last unit is keeping a balance between God's promise to himself and the more extended promises to every living thing so that the real climax comes in the section on the new world order and God's firm assurance in verse 17.

The narrator carries a heavy burden in the story of Noah and the flood. There is some dialogue at the beginning and the end of these chapters but it is all Yahweh's and is characterized by sharply contrasting moods. In the actual account of the flood there is no direct or indirect discourse, and the various aspects that we discussed above must be kept together in a unified progression. Awareness of the point of view and careful analysis of the style and climaxes are the keys to success in communicating this narrative to an audience.

There are innumerable other narratives in the Old Testament, but by and large they possess the same general characteristics as those we have discussed.

6
Narratives in the New Testament

Just as the Old Testament is in reality an extended and complex narrative tracing the history of a race, so the New Testament with the exception of Revelation may be said to trace the history of Christianity; but here the central interest is man rather than a nation. It is a story told from four points of view, each affected by the temperament of the narrator and by the milieu from which the writing came. It is quite probable that these accounts originally shared the oral tradition with the Old Testament, and thus much that we had to say in the previous section is equally applicable here. Moreover, both Books exhibit the intuitive mind and the capacity for wonder and immediate response. Both are characterized by concrete thinking and emotional undercurrent.

However, all four of the Gospels and indeed most of Acts have some common characteristics that set them apart from the Old Testament. We have said that much of the Old Testament is, technically speaking, biography. The Gospels do not fall so neatly into this category despite their focus on the life of Jesus. Neither are they strictly reminiscences. They are not primarily concerned with delineating a person but rather with establishing belief in the qualities that person displayed and thus proclaiming and publicizing the good news. There is no attempt to describe Jesus' appearance or voice; rather, his attitude and his symbolic gestures often serve us as description. The writers felt themselves to be the possessors of a tremendous fact, and their tone is one of announcement and proclamation without theory or elaboration or speculation.

In view of the general nature of the New Testament, arguments, long expositions, elaborate descriptions, or complex characterizations would be out of place. The style is simple and geared to the listeners the writers wished to reach. The time sequence is clear and chronological, with frequent references to "at that time," "the next day," "on another occasion," and so forth. Places are usually identified and carry with them much of the burden of association that we noted in the Old Testament.

The Gospels

Although the first three Gospels are so similar as to be termed "Synoptic," that is, "with one eye," there are some noticeable differences in writing style and in selectivity of details and episodes. Matthew, for example, is primarily concerned with the fulfillment of the law and the prophecies, and he relies heavily on frequent references to the Old Testament. His proclamation is of God as King of man and consequently with that segment of humanity which has at last come to know, love, and serve that King. His five books are made up of discourses introduced by carefully selected narrative materials.

Matthew is probably the most orderly of the four Gospel writers, and he provides the clearest organization with his topical grouping of blocks of material around a central theme. He is careful to supply connectives, especially of time and place progression. He is able to weave the many separate episodes into a connected chronological story. Jesus, the Prince of Israel, is always the focus, and Matthew does little developing of the disciples as individuals. He gives almost no space to Mary or Joseph, and his account of the birth of Jesus is crisply factual.

Mark's Gospel speaks repeatedly of the miraculous powers of the Messiah. As a disciple of Peter he often gives us glimpses of the personal experiences recounted by Peter in his preaching. His accounts are vividly realistic and emphasize the reactions of the general public and the crowds which followed Jesus. Thus with Mark we are often able to understand motivations and share responses more clearly despite the compactness and rapidity of his narratives. His frequent use of the historical present tense helps capture this immediacy for us. He is on the whole more conerned with the deeds of Jesus than with his words.

Luke, who authorities feel gained much of his information through personal inquiry, is a faithful reporter. His narratives are orderly and he appears to be interested in giving exact information. His focus is on the humanity within the divinity of Jesus and it is in his gospel that we find some wonderful touches of dignity and graciousness of the Messiah. Luke gives us the most detailed accounts of the many journeys and his references to the Holy City are frequent. He speaks with simplicity, but his use of Semitic idioms which are found, for example, in his account of the coming of Jesus, lend symbolism to the ceremonies and journeys he recounts. In fact it is from Luke that we get the human side of the genealogy of Jesus in contrast with Matthew's "table of descent."

John's interest goes beyond the fulfillment of the prophecy, the miraculous powers, and the love of mankind into a concern with Jesus' cosmic significance; his writings reflect a deeper apprehension of the mystery of the Word made flesh and sent to save mankind. He, too, proclaims Jesus as the Messiah but his teaching is aimed more directly at bringing men to this belief that they may attain life. He indicates more interest in worship and prayer. This is partly a result of the amount of time that had elapsed since Jesus' presence on earth and the beginning of the formalization of the early church. The things Jesus did were signs, and John points out the significance of these acts. His Gospel is a proclamation.

Types of Narrative

It is probably helpful to consider two groups of narratives in the New Testament. There are the teaching narratives in which we find Jesus speaking directly, as in the parables and his conversations with the disciples. Then there are the narratives told by the narrator of Jesus' travels, describing his cures and miracles, his sermons and various occasions and deeds. These, of course, need not be separated from the unity of the whole, but they present somewhat different problems to the interpreter.

We will deal first with the narrative episodes in which the actions and words of Jesus are reported to us in the person of the narrator. All four writers basically keep themselves and their personalities out of our way. All we need to know about the narrator and his attitude is probably revealed in his style and selection of details. Even in these units, however, there are usually some speeches of Jesus in direct discourse. It is interesting to note that they are almost identical in the four writings. This is probably due to the accepted "borrowing" from each other and from older sources and the unwillingness to presume to change what was originally attributed to Jesus.

There is a great deal of direct discourse in the New

Testament. The disciples and others speak often to Jesus
and he replies to them directly. The problem for the interpreter here is similar to that discussed in the handling of
the speeches of Yahweh in the Old Testament. Again we
do not know how Jesus sounded nor how he looked. We
only have reports of what he said and did. But from these
reports we know what kind of person he was. There was
great wisdom, compassion, and patience with those who
did not understand, and there were flashes of anger and
great strength. There is a subtle difference between the
way Jesus spoke to those individuals who came to ask his
help and to the crowds to whom he preached. Examine
the style carefully and you will be aware how it reflects
the intimacy in the first case and the clarity and simplicity
of forthrightness in the second. There is also a change
when Jesus is speaking to his disciples, whom he knew
well, whom he understood perfectly in their individual
strengths and weaknesses, and whom he loved.

God the father speaks directly and in his own person
less frequently in the New Testament than in the Old
Testament, but the interpreter would do the passage of
Jesus' baptism and the account of the transfiguration great
injustice if he failed to suggest the pride and love as God
speaks to and of his Son as "the Chosen One" and "the
Beloved."

These narrative units are not likely to give the interpreter a great deal of difficulty if he is aware of the climax
of each unit and takes care to make the direct discourse
stay within the total framework of the episode without
losing its vitality. The speeches of Jesus are usually brief
and simple and the situation itself usually suggests attitude. A comparative look at the four reports of the first
miracle of the loaves and fishes as they appear in *The New
English Bible* might prove interesting by way of illustra-
tion of the above comments.

Matthew (14:13–21) begins the account with "When he heard what had happened [the beheading of John the Baptist], Jesus withdrew privately by boat to a lonely place," indicating that his sorrow over the fate of John motivated his wish to be alone. Mark (6:30–45), on the other hand, attributes his desire for solitude to compassion for his weary disciples with "He said to them 'Come with me, by yourselves, to some lonely place where you can rest quietly.'" Luke (9:10–18) attributes no motivation to their withdrawal, saying only, "he took them [the apostles] with him and withdrew privately to a town called Bethsaida." He makes no mention of the boat referred to by Matthew and Mark. John begins simply with "Sometime later Jesus withdrew to the farther shore of the Sea of Galilee (or Tiberias), and a large crowd of people followed" (6:1–16). John also tells us that it was near the time of Passover and further identifies Andrew and Philip by name. He has Jesus asking Philip directly where he could buy bread for so many, and adds, "This he said to test him; Jesus himself knew what he meant to do" (6:6). Another interesting point of difference is that in John's account a boy in the crowd has the five barley loaves and two fishes whereas in the other accounts it is assumed that the provisions had been brought by the apostles.

Despite these differences, the facts are precisely the same, including the number of loaves and fishes, the number that were fed, and the amount which was gathered up after they had all eaten all they wanted. And the dialogue is essentially the same. In the narration Matthew and Mark tend to use somewhat longer and more syntactically complex sentences, while both Luke and John use shorter sentences of simpler construction. All four mention Jesus' compassion for the crowd and his patience in healing them (or teaching them, as Mark indicates).

Thus in every case there is the introduction, the heart

of the story which begins with the mention that it was getting late, and the conclusion which describes the gathering of fragments after the crowd was satisfied. John appends the additional conclusion of Jesus' fleeing because he knew the people would take him and make him king, but the story of the miracle itself ends with the twelve baskets of fragments.

Special Problems of the Narrator

It is in the teaching parables that the problem of direct discourse is intensified. Whether the words we are given are exactly those which Jesus spoke is, of course, impossible to tell. We work with what we are given. We have noted that the words of Jesus are very similar if not identical in the four Gospels so that we may certainly assume at least accuracy of spirit among the various versions and translations. It is here—in the spirit—that too many readers of scripture go astray.

In the first place there is an understandable reticence about trying to "pretend that you are Jesus." The matter of taste and reverence makes us reluctant to allow ourselves to identify fully with such a speaker. Thus we pull back and make him sound parroted and limp. He was obviously a vigorous man with great concern for reaching his listeners. Even when he was weary, as in the unit we have been discussing, his compassion for the crowds that followed him made him reach out to them. This *must* be at the core of our reading of his words.

A second problem in making Jesus' words come alive is their familiarity. We have heard them quoted—and misquoted—since we were children. The temptation is to treat them as quotations. They were not quotations when they were uttered. They were vital and fresh and sprang from a heart and mind which, while we cannot hope to match it, we can at least strive toward. It is essential that the reader re-create the situation in which the lessons were taught. This, of course, means re-creating the one-to-one or one-to-many basis of direct communication. He spoke to people, not to pews and pillars. And people responded with action and emotion.

The third problem is the fear of being theatrical. As we pointed out in an earlier chapter, one is only theatrical or "arty" when his attention is on himself and how he is performing. If he stands afar off and listens with awe to the beauty of his rolling tones, or turns his attention from what he is saying to execute a meticulously rehearsed gesture, we no longer believe what he is saying nor that he is speaking to us. That is being arty. When the mind is attending to what is being said and the reader's techniques are being used to support the demands of the material, and to share it fully with his listeners, there is very little danger of overstepping the bounds of decorum and good taste.

Careful analysis of style and organization will help to guide voice and body. An interesting example to look at in this respect is the parable of the sower (Luke 8:4-16; Matt. 13:1-24; Mark 4:1-21) which Jesus gave to the crowd of listeners who themselves worked the land and knew the way of seeds and growing. The crowd was so large that he got into a boat and spoke to them from there. His first sentence "A sower went out to sow," gets directly to what is relevant in their lives. It is short and simple. The repetition of "others" keeps their attention focused on the seeds as the parable progresses.

Later his apostles come to him and ask for an explanation of the parable. His tone and style change subtly as he speaks to the small intimate group to whom the faith had already been given. There are numerous such examples of style shifts that give clear clues as to attitude of the speaker toward his listeners, as well as the occasion and the size and background of the audience. An awareness of these clues will allow the interpreter to use his voice and body techniques effectively, to avoid monotony, and to resist the temptation to adopt a ministerial tone or pompously handle the simple and important parables. Indeed it is true that "a man's words flow out of what fills his heart" (Matt. 12:34); it behooves the interpreter of all literature to spend time analyzing so that he can be sure of the type of heart and mind that controlled the speeches and actions of the characters.

Analysis of the Passion and Death

Most of the narrative units of the New Testament are brief and simply organized. This eliminates some problems for the oral reader but intensifies others, such as the need to pinpoint the climaxes and make the abrupt transitions of time and place, or from introduction to core to conclusion, work effectively. There is, however, one extended narrative, of extreme importance to the Christian reader, which is usually done in its entirety. It is one of the most difficult units of the New Testament. We are referring, of course, to the account of the Passion and death of Jesus. A brief look at this section may serve to point out some of its difficulties.

Again the accounts of this climax of the New Testament differ somewhat from one Gospel to another. Matthew, Mark, and Luke make skillfull use of suspense, and we are led on a lingering and sorrowful journey to the fulfillment of the ancient prophecies. When properly read aloud so that the experience is shared, all three accounts are masterful. John, however, takes a somewhat different approach that needs very careful handling indeed but that for modern listeners carries a relevance which is equally moving.

John puts the Last Discourse into poetry, a style that fits the emotional intensity and the sweep and elevation of the content. The Passion proper begins with "After this discourse," which may be omitted if it seems confusing to the audience. But the interpreter will find it helpful to establish situation and attitude by remembering that Jesus has just broken bread and drunk wine with his apostles for the last time and bade them farewell. He is approaching the end of his mission on earth, an end for which he alone knows the purpose. The action that follows represents the culmination and realization of the words he has just spoken to them.

The Passion according to John comprises five major units in the two chapters. The first unit, which contains only eleven verses, serves as a general introduction and is packed with relevant information and references. It must not be hurried, although there are only two sentences to introduce this small section. Judas and his actions are mentioned immediately. Within the few verses there are valuable "stage directions." We will use the version found in The Anchor Bible, vol. 29a in the following illustrations.

When Jesus asks, "Whom are you looking for?" the question is prefaced by John's comment, "Knowing fully what was to happen to him, Jesus came out to them." Also, when Jesus identifies himself as the one they are seeking, we are told that "they stepped back and fell to the ground." Thus when Jesus asks his question a second time and they reply once more, "Jesus the Nazarene," the second answer would contain none of the bravado and authority of the first because they have been struck down by the presence they are confronting. Nevertheless, they parrot themselves because they are incapable of changing their plan.

The main story is interrupted immediately for John's comment on the fulfillment of a prophecy, and then we move at once into the minor episode of Peter and his sword. The conclusion of this unit is a single sentence telling us that Jesus was arrested and bound. The swiftness of this section is astonishing, despite the fact that the action is broken by what are in fact (and so noted in some translations) parenthetical explanations by the narrator.

The second major division (verses 12–27) is likewise brief and crowded with action: the interrogation before Annas, the identification of Annas, his interrogation of Jesus, the slap in the face, Jesus' being sent to Caiaphas, and Peter's three denials. Two scenes in separate settings are occurring simultaneously, and our attention is drawn alternately from inside the high priest's palace to the courtyard where Peter and numerous others are warming themselves over a charcoal fire and talking among themselves. Although it is not made specifically clear, the assumption is that Peter is alone among strangers who are none too friendly. There is also a definite time progression to be made clear.

It is no simple task for the interpreter to keep all of these aspects unified and moving in the proper channels. The problem is further complicated when we realize that the scene in each setting has its own separate climax. Peter's is, in a way, a climax of character development, reached when he makes his third denial, but we are most moved by the cock's crow which was foretold only a few hours before. The climax of the interrogation taking place inside is probably the blow on the cheek, partly because it is unexpected.

Some knowledge of Jewish law and the recollection of Yahweh's saying in Isaiah 45:19, "I have said nothing in secret," will help keep Jesus' speeches from sounding arrogant, as they might to the modern ear. He was replying with dignity and was well within his rights when he asked, "Why do you question me?" (18:21) for the Jewish law held that it was improper for an accused person to convict himself. Thus the proper procedure would have been to question those who had heard him.

This is a difficult unit and its effectiveness will depend to a large extent on the interpreter's ability to concentrate on characters in specific situations within both scenes without losing sight of the structuring of the two chapters as a unit.

It is interesting that John gives us no report on the interrogation before Caiaphas nor does he mention the Sanhedrin meeting which the other three Gospels cover. Thus he compensates in speed and sharpness of focus for what he loses in suspense, and the third unit (18:28–19:16) opens with "Now, at daybreak, they took Jesus from Caiaphas to the praetorium. They did not enter the praetorium themselves, for they had to avoid ritual impurity in order to be able to eat the Passover supper. So Pilate came out to them." Thus the scene is set.

This unit is remarkable for its organization and rhythm. Its seven episodes alternate perfectly between outside, where Pilate came to meet Jesus and his captors, and inside, where Pilate conducts his trial. But this time there is no real problem of unity between the two settings because Pilate himself takes us back and forth. John is explicit with such connective devices as "Pilate went out again," "Once more Pilate went out," "Going back into the praetorium," and finally, "Then, at last, Pilate handed Jesus over to them to be crucified."

Pilate emerges with startling clarity in John's version of the trial. We are given a glimpse of a professional politician caught between two forces: the one, his reason,

which finds no guilt in the accused man and makes him
reluctant to get involved in his death; the other, we might
term public pressure and mob reaction. In his first conversation with Jesus we sense a respect for and curiosity
about his prisoner. He addresses him as one of equal intelligence and reasonableness. There is also a touch of impatience as if this were one more problem to be coped
with in his life full of irritating confrontations and pres-
sures. This one differs from the others only in the obvious
caliber of the accused man and the disturbing claims to
kingship (which would enrage Caesar and thus put
Pilate's position in jeopardy) and to being the Son of God.

Pilate's questions to Jesus are direct and seem to give
him every opportunity to extricate himself and thus spare
Pilate the necessity of solving the problem. Pilate quite
accurately points out that he is not a Jew and that it was
Jesus' own countrymen who brought him. His direct questions are "Are you 'the King of the Jews'?" "What have
you done?" "So, then, you are a king?" and "Truth? . . .
And what is that?" One could not ask for a more straight-
forward approach. The last question hints at a sophisticated cynicism that has grown out of his long political
career. He is equally direct in his confrontation with the
Jews, saying, when he realizes they cannot be moved by
persuasion, "I find no case against him."

The fourth unit also moves swiftly to its climax, the
crucifixion. Only two sentences tell us that they took
custody of Jesus, that he carried the cross himself, arrived
at "the Place of the Skull," and that he was crucified along
with two others. We hear no more about the two thieves
in John's version. Next we have the inscription and Pilate's
terse comment when the Jews objected, "What I have
written, I have written."

John uses the interlude before Jesus' actual death to

bring our attention down from the cross to where the soldiers are "tossing" for the seamless tunic and then to the small group of women. The humanity of Jesus is beautifully pointed in his concern for the future of his mother. But our attention is not distracted from the cross and John brings us back firmly with "After this, aware that all was now finished, in order to bring the Scripture to its complete fulfillment," and we have the request for a drink. Jesus' last words are particularly telling in John's Gospel. Matthew and Mark tell us he uttered a loud cry but do not give us any words. Luke has him address his last words directly to the Father. John gives us a simple statement that the long ministry and all the weight of prophecies have now been accomplished and "he handed over his spirit."

The denouement of the tests for death and the prophecies thus fulfilled, the descent from the cross and the burial are handled swiftly. The closing sentence may seem abrupt and unfeeling unless the reader has kept the whole tone of the account firmly in mind. There is, however, a particularly human and ironic twist in it. The business was over and no more could be done. And there was no time to quibble because of the Jewish Day of Preparation. "And so . . . they buried Jesus in this nearby tomb." The use of his name instead of the pronoun (19:42) brings the narrative to a quiet and final close.

Close analysis and careful preparation are needed to make this extended narrative come alive for us again. It is a difficult one to handle but is basically so moving and so relevant that, done with care, there is an added level of identity for modern listeners. To negate or fail to utilize all the dramatic and narrative qualities in this account, whether it be John's or from the Synoptic Gospels, is to impede full communication, which in terms of sharing the

Bible is the height of egocentricity. God gave us minds, voices, bodies, and responses. He certainly expects us to use them fully in proclaiming his message.

The Acts of the Apostles

The Acts of the Apostles, which completes the narratives in the New Testament, is a highly episodic narrative about the primitive church and apostles. Each chapter has its own set of characters and its own organization. Johannes Munck describes the Acts well when he explains that, "To read Acts through from beginning to end is like travelling in mountainous Switzerland, a land sharply divided into separate areas which has nevertheless been molded into a whole both by nature and by human effort." [1]

Although lacking the essential unity of the presence of Jesus which characterizes the Gospels, the Acts of the Apostles is not likely to give the interperter much difficulty. The episodes partake of the general characteristics of all narratives. The unifying principle is the recounting of the progress of the mission assumed by the apostles. There are interesting sidelights on their individuality and an especially rich section dealing with Paul's missionary work which could certainly have been drawn from direct knowledge.

Acts is probably not to be taken as an historical document but rather as a kind of *apologia* tracing the development of the new religion and incidentally designed to convince the Romans that the new Christians were not hostile to their laws and therefore should not be persecuted. It also reveals how the teaching of the faith in

1. The Anchor Bible. (New York: Doubleday, 1967), vol. 31, p. xxviii.

Christ became gradually more precise although the date and place of writing are unclear. The interpreter would do well to review our few remarks on Luke's style in the Gospel, although Luke actually mixes styles more freely in the Acts. Attention to the by now familiar process of style and organization analysis will reveal a good deal of variety within the essential unity of purpose and intended readership.

7

Epistles

In examining the sections of biblical literature that may be classified as "non-narrative," it is extremely difficult to formulate any tight and indisputable categories. The complexity and combination of writing techniques found in the books of both Testaments place a tremendous demand on the interpreter. Nevertheless, he must be cognizant of the differences between a selection which is built primarily around a narrative chronological unity and that writing which uses quite another method of organization to achieve its unity, the Epistle. The chronological narrative may teach a lesson by telling what happened to whom, but the Epistle relies on a different type of word choice and syntax to achieve its purpose of clarification, instruction, correction, or persuasion.

We are fully aware of current research which calls into question the authorship of many of the Epistles, but for our purposes we shall assume that the letters credited to Paul were written or dictated by him and those credited to or seemingly signed by John were written by him, and so forth. This assumption does not represent slipshod scholarship on our part, since we are concerned with the role of the interpreter. The interpreter must, as we have said, make use of all that the textual scholars have discovered, but he is not concerned at the moment with recreating the physical and occupational characteristics of the writer but with the literature itself.

Any writer will alter his style to some extent to suit the purpose of the letter he is writing and the interests and relationship of the addressee. So, if Paul did not write all the letters credited to him, and if John, whose letters are so designated was not really named John or if he was not the same John who wrote the Gospel, the interpreter must concern himself with what is on the printed page and simply accept the fact that someone named something wrote in such and such a manner, and that the letters are authentic for a time and place. The interpreter makes himself the embodiment and transmitter of the letter, not of the physical exterior characteristics or the biography of the writer.

The Epistles are messages directed to a specific audience of one or many. They are written or dictated by someone in a particular set of circumstances and sent to another or others with whom the writer is acquainted or at least about whom he has some relevant information. Thus both the writer, as we find him through an examination of his style, and the intended recipients whom he is addressing in that style, must be taken into consideration in preparation for reading the messages aloud. The quotations in the following discussion are taken from The Jerusalem Bible.

Corinthians

Although Paul's Letter to the Romans is considered by many to be his masterpiece, let us continue to examine his First Letter to the Corinthians which is perhaps more familiar to the layman and thus may stand in even greater need of being revitalized in its performance. In Chapter Three we looked at it very briefly and noted its general principles of organization and unification. We noted also Paul's use of "we" and "you and I" as well as the opening and closing statements of his position in relation to the addressees and his affection and concern for them as followers of Jesus. We also looked briefly at the grouping of ideas and the transitions from one to the other. This letter is, of course, one of Paul's "public" letters, meant to be shared with all the faithful in Corinth.

It is interesting to distinguish between private and public letters in the Epistles. Those written by Paul to Timothy, for example, fall more easily into the category of private letters, or at least "open" letters addressed to one person but intended to be shared by others; the tone is informal and affectionate, and the organization is dictated partially by the close relationship which Paul felt with the younger man. The bulk of the Epistles, however, were public letters. They were sent to a leader of a group to be shared with the faithful, probably in a public assembly. Thus they have both epistolary and rhetorical characteristics, and some are very close to orations in their method of organization and adaptability for a large audience

As the First Letter to the Corinthians progresses, one feels Paul must have had before him not only the letters he is answering but also a complete list of actual and possible transgressions. He moves clearly and directly from one error to another, always returning to the Corinthians' privileged position, their knowledge of truth, and an implied confidence in their strength. Almost without exception, the various units end with an expression of his own affection for them and thus a return to his opening note of unity and harmony among them. The method of transition from one major unit of thought into another is usually simple and candid. Often he seems to be simply saying in effect, "Now, the next thing on my list is . . . ," but the careful reader will notice that the ideas are grouped so that they fall into related categories.

First there is incest, which is considered to be even worse than the practices of the pagans, then recourse to the pagan courts, then fornication, followed by a discussion of marriage and virginity. The discussion of food offered to the idols is indeed a break and depends for continuity upon its connection to the pagan practices, which by implication are compared to Christian wisdom and conduct discussed earlier. Next the pagan gifts are compared with spiritual gifts, and this leads directly to a consideration of love. The letter then develops the claims of love and the control which love places upon freedom. Paul then uses himself as an example to expand this theory of freedom and the necessity for disciplining the body. After recalling a lesson from history and a warning, he returns to a statement of his trust that God will not tax us beyond our strength. He again takes up the symbol of food and moves very easily into the further discussion of idols foreshadowed in 8:1.

The next step involves decorum in public worship that befits those who are *not* pagans but rather followers of Jesus, whose Supper is being celebrated. This, of course, leads most naturally into a discussion of spiritual gifts and the focus on their unity of source rather than on a separation of talents and faculties or on pride in their possession. This brings us to the justly famous and beautifully constructed unit on the importance of love as a greater gift than any of the others. After a word on the gift of prophecy, Paul gives a final word on the regulation of all spiritual gifts. Chapter 15, which concerns itself with the question of resurrection of the dead, returns to the opening statements of Jesus' death on the cross for its proof. The manner of resurrection is discussed, and the conclusion is the hymn of triumph.

Having disposed of matters of discipline and spiritual behavior, Paul concludes the letter with a few practical matters, returning to the opening tone of affection for these special people whom he will visit soon; he recommends Timothy to them as "doing the Lord's work" asking that he be welcomed by them, and he finally asks their charity for the Stephanas family who "have worked hard to help the saints." The letter ends as it began, with declarations of his special love for the receivers to whom he has referred often as "brothers" and "dearest children."

The Second Letter to the Corinthians is less clearly organized and it is thought by some to contain fragments of an earlier lost letter. Despite its lack of clear organization, it contains the interesting stylistic aspects of which Paul was a master. It leans heavily, however, toward apocalyptic imagery in several places, a rare occurence in Paul's other letters. There are units of a most powerful and rhetorically polished style, such as 1:12–6:10 in which the oratorical devices are brilliantly used. And then, lest he perhaps lose the less sophisticated members of his audience, he reverts to a warmer, more intimate, informal style. His "Apologia" (chapters 10–13) is strong and forceful, with a vocabularly that brooks no nonsense or misunderstanding.

Galatians and Romans

Galatians and Romans deal with essentially the same problem and are often paried in discussions. There are, however, some very sharp differences between them. The Letter to the Galatians appears to be Paul's immediate reaction to a situation. He mixes personal and emotional appeals (1:12–2:21) with doctrinal arguments (3:1–4:31) and earnest and direct "I–you" admonitions (5:1–6:17). His last sentence lacks the affection and warmth we have come to expect from him and merely says, "The grace of our Lord Jesus Christ be with your spirit, my brothers. Amen." Throughout he blends short, abrupt questions and answers with longer, more involved sentences explaining and expanding the questions and answers. The rhythm has a strong beat with numerous examples of clustered stresses. It is the type of letter that would reach anyone who is guilty and serve as a deterrent to those who might be entertaining any ideas of straying!

Letter to the Romans, on the other hand, is indeed a masterpiece in both organization and style. It will be remembered that Paul did not himself found the Roman church, and his information about the Romans is less complete than his firsthand knowledge of the Galatians. He is addressing a mixed community in which there were developing some tension and snobbism between the Jewish and non-Jewish members. He is preparing them, as well as himself, for his visit to them, and part of the letter serves as an authentication of his position and authority. The whole letter is carefully planned and phrased, even its introduction, which outlines what is to follow.

There are numerous rhetorical questions which he answers in short direct statements. Twice in the early part of the letter he asks, "Does this mean . . .?" and replies firmly to his own question, "Of course not" (6:16 and 7:7). There are numerous carefully documented quotations from scripture and specific references to David, Abraham, Rebecca, Moses, Pharaoh, Hosea, and Isaiah—a very subtle piece of audience adaptation. There are sentences which might well serve as maxims and stand as quotations after the letter had been read, such as "God has no favorites" (2:11), and "God never takes back his gifts or revokes his choice" (11:29). In several places he ends a unit of thought with "Amen" (1:25, 9:5, 11:36, 15:31, 16:27).

This letter perhaps comes closer to an oration than any of the others. It is a more formal communication than the Letter to the Galatians, for example. Paul has assembled his ideas of God and stated them more precisely than was necessary in writing those whom he had already taught in person and who were familiar with his personality and dedication. In some ways it resembles the modern communication from the Bishop to the priests and laity, and sparingly employs the persuasive factors of the "we . . . you and I" relationship. His discussion of the Law, which is referred to often in the letter, is certainly explanatory, but there is no hint that they have not understood its basic premises.

The whole letter carries a tone of authority and dignity. It contains numerous exalted expostulations, and the phrase, "through Jesus Christ our Lord" appears frequently, especially after the early chapters, while in the other letters he usually says simply, "Christ" or "Christ Jesus." Also in a large proportion of the references to Jesus, his name is carefully linked with that of God the Father, as in "may God our Father and the Lord Jesus Christ send you grace and peace" (1:7), "Thanks be to God through Jesus Christ our Lord!" (7:24), "heirs of God and cohorts with Christ" (8:17), and "give glory to the God and Father of our Lord Jesus Christ" (15:6), for example. He is careful to establish Christ's divinity with such statements as "Christ who is above all, God forever blessed" (9:5), and several other similar references, but Romans is heavily laced with references to "God" in contrast to the emphasis of "Christ" in the other letters.

Stylistic Elements

Let us, for contrast, analyze three of the more intimate "private" letters, 1 Timothy, 2 Timothy, and Titus. Looking first at the salutations, one immediately notices a difference in word choice within the seemingly standard format. In Corinthians the salutation is formal, beginning "I, Paul," and continuing "send greetings to the church of God." The prayer for them, "May God our Father and our Lord Jesus Christ send you grace and peace," has the phrasing of a formal benediction. We have mentioned the salutation in Romans with its authentication and outline of what is to come. In Galatians he reminds the receivers immediately that his authority is from God, not from man.

Both salutations to Timothy are less extended and warmer in tone. Both begin simply, "From Paul," and continue "to Timothy, true child of mine in faith," or, in the case of 2 Timothy, the even more intimate "dear child of mine." The first sentence moves without terminal punctuation into the informal "wishing you grace, mercy and peace." There is no inserted comment on faith, doctrine, or behavior. The blessing is direct and simple, and "wishing you" has an intimacy totally lacking in the more formal "May God . . . send you . . ."

The greeting to Titus falls somewhere between the two described above. It uses the "From . . . To . . ." format, but between them lies one of Paul's characteristic "sermonettes" and a statement of his position and mission. However, he again uses "true child of mine in the faith" and the verb "wishing."

The conclusions to the four letters continue to reflect the differing relationships between writer and receivers. Corinthians uses eight short sentences, with the words "greetings," "greeting," and "greet" appearing in three of them. There is, of course, also "warmest wishes" and "love . . . in Christ Jesus," but the greetings, wishes, and love are clearly those of Christian leader for a group of Christians rather than of one person for another. And there is also the pastoral warning, "If anyone does not love the Lord, a curse on him. '*Maran atha.*'" [1]

The conclusion to 1 Timothy begins with "My dear Timothy," which is followed by the admonition to avoid certain types of discussions and knowledge; it ends with the simple "Grace be with you." The Second Letter to Timothy ends with greetings from Prisca and Aquila and the family of Onesiphorus and news of Erastus and Trophimus. This is followed by the direct and intimate "Do your best to come before winter," then more personal greetings, and the closing sentences, "The Lord be with your spirit. Grace be with you" (4:22).

You will recall that in Chapter Three mention was made of the importance of the salutation and closing as determinants of the tone of the entire letter. Even when only a small excerpt from the letter is being used, it is important to adhere to the tone and degree of intimacy indicated in the opening and closing sections as a guide to the relationship of writer to addressees; attention to tone will also help in evaluating and comprehending the persuasive appeals used throughout.

Even a brief look at the word choice in these four Epistles will reveal that there is consistency and harmony between the openings and closings within the body of each of the letters. Within 1 Corinthians, the words are strong and carry the tone of a leader and teacher. Some of them are "witnesses," "gifts of the Spirit," "the last day," "I appeal," "brothers," "my dear brothers," "preach," "salvation," "oratory," "philosophy," "guaranteed," "knowl-

1. Our Lord is come.

edge," "foolishness," "boast," "servants," "stewards," "bring you to your senses," to mention only a few. These are authoritative words and must be spoken with confidence and strength, tempered always by the affection and "we" concept which is so carefully established and returned to at frequent intervals.

The word choice throughout the two letters to Timothy forms a striking contrast to 1 Corinthians. Here we have "As I asked you," "I ask you to remember," "My advice is," "I am reminding you," "Remind them," "You know," "You are well aware," "Do your best to come," "When you come, bring the cloak," "something precious," and the list of qualities of a presiding officer which include "temperate," "impeccable," "discreet," "kind," "peaceable," and so forth. Toward the end of the second letter, starting in chapter 3, there are numerous words of courage and strength such as "confidence," "good soldier," "athlete," "rules of the contest," "dedicated," "ready," "duty," "insist," "brave," "good fight," "power," which reflect the strength of the writer despite his imprisonment and his certainty of equal strength in Timothy.

The word choice in Titus is even simpler and indicates a patient willingness to explain and clarify: "The reason," "You see," "Remember," "I want you to be," "behavior," "instructions," "lose no time in joining me." Although some of the advice given in this letter parallels that given to Timothy, the diction is much simpler, a fact which may reflect his attitude either toward Titus, whom he knew well and in whom he had great confidence, or more likely toward the group with whom Titus would probably share the letter. The reason behind the simplicity is of less importance to the interpreter than the presence of these words and shorter, more direct sentences on the page.

The rhythm of 1 Corinthians varies, of course, with the content of each paragraph and the force of Paul's admonitions, but in general there are frequent short sentences which usually clearly direct the receivers to "do" or "do not," carry out something concerning an item of faith or a standard of conduct. Several of them are rhetorical questions which will force the listeners to an answer clearly designated by what Paul has taught them and by the proof offered in Jesus' death for them. The longer sentences are characteristically packed and often present a balance between two factors so that in oral performance they separate into nearly equal segments.

Often the stresses cluster or group into a falling rhythm, as in the following questions where the falling rhythm words are italicized:

> *Isn't* that *obvious* from all the *jealousy* and *wrangling* that there is among you, from the way you go on behaving like *ordinary people*? What could be more *unspiritual* than your *slogans*, "I am for Paul" and "I am for Appolos" (3.3)?

It is interesting that this "pounding rhythm" and the pairing of strong stresses almost disappears in the sections on the resurrection, except in a few instances such as the reprimand,

> Come to your senses, behave properly, and leave sin alone (15:34).

The two letters to Timothy have many long flowing sentences. The stressed words are usually separated by several which need not be stressed, and the rhythm is gentle. The following sentence is a good example of this rhythm, and it is interesting that the only place where the stresses are paired is in the phrase, "God's family. . . ." The sentence itself and all the phrases within it start with one or two unstressed syllables.

> At the moment of writing to you, I am hoping that I may be with you soon; but in case I should be delayed, I wanted you to know how people ought to behave in God's family (1 Timothy 3:14–15).

And even when Paul is speaking with great gravity, as in 2 Timothy 1:7–14, there is still the gentle rhythm:

> God's gift was not a spirit of timidity, but the Spirit of power, and love, and self-control. . . . You have been trusted to look after something precious; guard it with the help of the Holy Spirit who lives in us.

The only two incidents of paired stresses occur, appropriately enough, on "God's gift" and "look after."

In Titus the rhythm varies more markedly and rapidly than it does in the letters to Timothy. This is obviously consistent with the content as Paul speaks quietly and gently to Titus in the early part of the letter, explaining and reminding him of certain matters:

> The reason I left you behind in Crete was for you to get everything organized there and appoint elders in every town, in the way I told you (1:15).

Here again the sentence and each phrase within it start with one or more light stresses. However, very soon Paul begins to lay down rules or restate principles that he wishes Titus to relay to his followers to be actively carried out. At these points the strong rhythms and close proximity of stresses reflect the teacher making a point, clearly and forcefully.

The interpreter is certainly not going to go through the entire Bible and mark every syllable which will receive a stress! The above markings were merely intended to graphically represent to the interpreter a factor which already exists in the writing and which he should use to his advantage. Since he will practice reading the bulk of his work aloud in preparation for his performances, his ear will soon learn to catch the rhythmic patterns as they affect and are affected by the tone and implication of the content. Attitude of the writer toward the intended reader or listeners influences the length of sentences, the choice of words, the syntax, and certainly the rhythm of the writing.

Although we have looked only at the writings of Paul, examination of the rest of the Epistles will provide equally helpful clues for preparation and performance. James, in his letter to the twelve tribes, for example, uses a polished style which features many of the Hebraisms and parallel constructions with which his addressees are familiar and which will call to mind the early teachings of the Old Testament. This letter has the formality of a sermon for the most part and depends for much of its persuasive (or perhaps didactic) power on a tradition that serves to draw the emigrants closer together and to their faith.

Special Problems for the Interpreter

Each of the Epistles, and indeed all literature of all kinds, will provide many aids for the interpreter who will take the time and effort to examine it carefully. Analysis of elements such as we have been discussing here will help him retain unity without loss of variety within that unity, and will influence pace, use of pauses, emphasis, and vocal quality; it will also help him to use his techniques to best serve the material he has chosen and to communicate it fully to his audience.

Although the modern interpreter has examined and analyzed his selection from the Epistles thoroughly and, with the help of biblical scholars and historians, has determined the writer, recipient, and circumstances of the letter, he may still be troubled with the problem of adapting the letter or excerpts from it to a modern audience. Solving this problem is more difficult in theory than it is in actual practice.

To begin with, he must fully identify with the writer. He must think as a person would think within the given set of circumstances and given relationship to the recipient or recipients. Paul, for instance, was a leader and a teacher. His had been the task of conversion and his is the responsibility of helping his converts follow the teachings he had given them and retain the faith they had embraced. This is a serious matter to Paul and he writes as a spiritual father, confessor, adjudicator and interpreter of the law, as well as friend and fellow struggler with the distractions and temptations of the world. He will often adopt several of these roles in succession within a single letter, as we have seen. He is intelligent, earnest, deeply inspired, frank in his self-evaluation, firm in his beliefs, and informed about the state of affairs which he is discussing. He is enthusiastic and his mind goes quickly from one important matter to another, often balancing opposites and drawing a conclusion. Above all, he has great energy and a sense of dedication. The interpreter must believe as Paul believes, at least at the moment of performance. He must not imply ideas of his own by subordinating key thoughts and climaxes. It is Paul's letter, and the interpreter must adapt to whatever he finds there.

When the Epistles were written, each writer had an audience in mind, in many cases probably clearly visualized in its environment. His thoughts went *to* that place and those people as he wrote. When the interpreter is reading the letter in performance, he will find it helpful to make his modern audience analogous in some respects to the originally intended group of individuals. The precepts are still sound, and human beings have not changed as much as we might wish they had over the centuries. Therefore when using a selection from Corinthians the interpreter speaks in Paul's words, with the attitude discovered in the writing, to a group of interested and concerned listeners. Within a church service the motivation for their listening will be much the same as that of the Corinthians who gathered together to receive advice and admonition to help them obtain their goal. When the material is used purely as literature, an appreciative audience may likewise be assumed.

The familiarity of the material and generations of bad readings of it must be compensated for by careful attention to focal points, climaxes, lead-ins and conclusions of individual units, and all the other factors discovered in analysis. Forthrightness and vitality of thought are essential. The audience or "addressees" are modern Corinthians (although perhaps somewhat less recalcitrant) or a group of Timothys or Tituses. There must be direct eye contact which results from direct mental contact and the intent to share the material completely. There are numerous sections which may be classified among the great orations of history. They contain all the rhetorical devices of the classic orators, and a careful examination of style is imperative in dealing with them.

There is so much to be said about the Epistles that scholars have written volumes on a single letter. This chapter has only touched on a few general points. Every letter and indeed every chapter of every letter has its variations, its particular challenges of style and organization, and its prevailing tone and attitude. The attempt here has been only to remind the interpreter that these writings are too complex to be read without careful preparation, which entails a painstaking look at every detail in order that he may use his voice and body to communicate them fully.

8
Poetry in the Bible

One of the most difficult tasks of the literary critic is to come up with a definition of poetry that pleases both poets and readers! Some prose comes so close to having the qualities of poetry that belaboring the distinction becomes a waste of time. Poetry, as everyone knows, is writing arranged in short lines down the page; it sometimes rhymes; when we reach high school it has to be scanned. But that definition is no more satisfying than the long, elaborate treatises compiled by critics from the time of Aristotle to the present.

Nevertheless, for convenience of discussion we will follow the more simplistic designation and consider as poetry any unit which "is arranged in short lines down the page." And in so doing, we are immediately confronted with the difficult problems of editorship and translation which we mentioned in an earlier chapter. It is interesting and a little disconcerting to note that relatively little of the King James version is set in poetic form, yet its rhythmic pulse is one of its greatest appeals. Many modern translators obviously have found the elements of emotional content and sound pattern so strong in the Bible that they have used poetic typography.

Actually the basic difference between poetry and prose is one of degree. Broadly speaking, poetry differs from prose in the emotional weight of its content and the importance of its sound pattern. In poetry, perhaps more than in any other kind of literature, the content and the form are inseparable in achieving the total effect. One intensifies the other. A poet's ear is attuned to the sound of words as a composer's is to tone and the effect of tone sequences; the poet tests his words for sound as well as for denotation and connotation. Consequently, poetry may be said to be the particular province of the oral interpreter because it reaches its ultimate objective only when it is read aloud.

The emotional level of the content of poetry is heightened by its rhythmic elements and its figures of speech, such as similes and metaphors, which appeal to our senses and thus increase our empathic response. Poetry reaches its full meaning, a meaning which lies beyond fact, only when there is a perfect blend of sound and sense, each intensifying and enriching the other.

There is relatively little poetry in the New Testament, and what we do find is usually excerpted from the Old Testament to establish the continuum of history. For instance, Matthew in his account of the visit of the Magi and of the flight into Egypt (2::13–18) inserts four lines from Micah (5:1) and five lines from Jeremiah (35:15), recalling the earlier prophecies. The entire Gospel contains numerous such insertions. Mark uses fewer poetic sections but does open his Gospel with five poetic lines; he uses four lines from Isaiah when speaking of the traditions of the Pharisees (7:7); he quotes from Psalm 118:22–23 in 12:11 and from Psalm 110:1 in 12:11, 36. Luke, too interweaves poetry through his prose, and John's "Prologue" assumes poetic form in some modern versions. In fact, in several of the new translations about one-third of

John's account is printed in poetic form. And even Paul, whose *forte* was clear and logical prose, uses poetry when he wishes to appeal to the emotions. But the Old Testament presents us with the richest store of poetic expression, and we shall devote most of our attention to that writing, remembering that wherever poetry is found it requires particular attention from the interpreter.

Poetry is a record of an emotional experience to be shared. This does not mean that an experience must be explained, nor does it always suggest a totality of experience. A poet may share only a segment of his experience, translatable into terms of the reader's own experiences. He may certainly write of facts, but he interprets them in a larger sense. He may have been motivated by an "idea"; but if the "idea" had been his whole concern, he would not have needed the additional dimensions and richness of sound which are characteristic of poetry. He is usually concerned rather with an emotional or aesthetic response to the idea. Even in didactic poetry, where the idea is probably of primary importance, the provoking of emotive response is the poet's driving force. Sometimes the poet's intention is primarily to express and give aesthetic pleasure; or he may wish merely to create a mood of excitement or repose, or to recapture the effects of a specific emotion, such as love, hate, joy, or fear. In any case, he will go beyond the confines of strictly logical content. If the poet had wished simply to inform, he would have put his idea into prose—that is, into a form which lends itself much more easily to development of a purely logical idea. But the poet intends to communicate something beyond fact or opinion. Indeed, much poetry does not require an opinion at all. It asks of the reader merely the acceptance of an attitude—and considerable control of technique on the part of the oral communicator.

The first step in understanding and evaluating any piece

of literature is, of course, reading it over in its entirety to get a general idea of what it says. And this is the first thing to be done with a poem. This first step may be less objective, less purely "mental," with poetry, however, than with most prose or even with drama. The initial response to a poem may not be in terms of ideas or logical content at all, but rather in terms of pleasure or pain, activity or repose—in short, of emotive content. The interpreter should read the poem aloud—several times over—and permit himself the luxury of a completely subjective response before beginning the objective analysis. He should give full play to the sound and to the harmony between content and form. Instead of beginning at once to work on the poem, he should let the poem work on him for a while.

All the aspects of literary style are found in poetry as well as in prose. Syntax is often complicated and needs careful handling for clear understanding of relationships between verb forms and compound subjects or objects, for example. Sometimes the normal word order of a sentence is altered for emphasis or rhythmic value. Sentence length is of somewhat less importance in poetry than in prose, however, because of the contribution of the line as a unit of both thought and sound. There is even a special designation for the line-end. If the terminal syllable is accented, the line is said to have a masculine ending, as in "thrŏughóut thĕ eárth!" If the last syllable of the line has a lighter stress, as in "ŏf the ócĕăn," the ending is called feminine. But in general the principles we discussed in Chapter Three are applicable to all forms of writing. As a matter of fact the condensation of poetry, one of its chief characteristics, results in an even greater need to be aware of the aspects of literary style and to use them fully.

This condensation is achieved in part by extensive use of similes, metaphors, and personifications—devices we mentioned in Chapter Three. Such lines as "The Lord is thy shade upon thy right hand" (Ps. 121:5, King James), "your name like perfume poured out" (The Song of Songs 1:3, The New English Bible), "I am poured out like water . . . my heart is like wax . . . my strength is dried up like a potsherd" (Ps. 22:14–15, King James), "he is a buckler to all those that trust in him" (Ps. 18:30, King James), and "his truth shall be thy shield and buckler" (Ps. 91:4 King James), are excellent examples, and there are dozens of others with which we are familiar. The Song of Songs is particularly rich in similes and metaphors, and almost every unit revolves around a comparison that appeals heavily to a combination of senses and resultant muscle responses.

Organization

Poems have introductions, bodies, and conclusions, just as other pieces of writing, but the first and last are often so compact as to be almost exclamations or ejaculations. This is certainly true of Psalm 8, which we will look at in some detail later in this chapter, and which opens with

> O Lord our sovereign,
> how glorious is thy name in all the earth!
> The New English Bible

or, in the King James version:

> O Lord, our Lord,
> how excellent is thy name in all the earth!

The conclusion is an exact repetition of the opening lines.

Poems also have climaxes or high points of emotion. They often come swiftly and are heavy with sense and muscle appeals. In speaking of prose earlier, especially narrative prose, we mentioned the crisis, which is the point at which the story turns. In a poem this is called the *fulcrum*. It may be a single word or an entire unit, but it is the point at which the poem turns or balances. It may or may not coincide with the climax. For instance, in Psalm 23 there is a clear turn at verse 4 from quiet meditation to direct prayer of joy and thanksgiving with the shift from the third person to second person.

> He will lead me into luxuriant pastures,
> as befits his name.
> Even though I should walk
> in the midst of total darkness,
> I shall fear no danger
> since you are with me.
>
> (Ps. 23:3–4, The Anchor Bible)

Sometimes the turn may be from rightness to evil, or from night to morning, or oppression to relief, despair to hope in Yahweh, or even as simple as from down (in the depths or simply on this earth) to up, by a lifting of the eyes, the heart, the hands or the thoughts to the hill or the heavens beyond. The fulcrum is not always as clearly evident in biblical poetry as in more modern poetry, but an awareness of its presence can help immeasurably in retaining unity and building to the climax.

Just as the Bible as a whole contains a wide variety of types and styles of writing, the poetry of the Bible covers every type from dirges to hymns of joy and praise, and from narratives to love songs. There are anthems and odes, songs and meditations, prayers of hope and of suffering and of faith in the midst of adversity. Sometimes, indeed, a poem will begin as a lyric and yet carry within it a strong narrative thread, or vice versa. Within the Psalms, for instance, it is impossible to establish a thread of continuity from one to another which exists for very long at one time. One of the clearest and most extended is probably Psalms 120–134, where the pilgrimage to the sacred feast and then out of exile is traced from the beginning of deliverance through the family songs to the dedication of the Temple and finally to the departure from the Temple. Nevertheless it is probably best to consider the Psalms as separate poems as we will do in this chapter.

Most authorities now feel that there is no indisputable identity of the speaker or singer of these beautiful poems. However, it is helpful to attempt to clarify the speaker, usually called the *persona*, in the poems of the Bible. This is not to say that his exact name or station or his physical size or the color of his hair must be identified but rather whether he is speaking for all his people or for himself and under what circumstances. If he is one of the prophets, he will be relating what Yahweh said to him under a vital compulsion to share it with a chosen group. In Song of Songs there are three speakers, the bride, the bridegroom, and the chorus or single speaker who handles the transitional units. Obviously their attitudes and points of view are not identical, and the stylistic aspects with which we are now so familiar will serve as a guide to degree of involvement in the emotional experience being shared. Lamentations is spoken by a persona who uses both third and first person discourse, and in most cases the first person can be taken as speaking not of himself but of a people and, in a sort of "reverse personification," of the city as well. The Psalms mix first person and third person personae at will, and again the first person does not always indicate a personal, individual "I," but rather a spokesman for the many. He is an ideal person with deep knowledge of the past and hope in Yahweh, and the circumstances of which he sings are universal for his time and people. Even the confessions of guilt and fear and despair carry this universality, whether it be the experience of one or many.

Word Choice

One of the aspects of style which may bear a closer look in poetry is that of word choice. As we have said, a poet chooses his words for their sound and their connotation as well as for their dictionary meaning. Sound and connotation become extremely important in the emotive force in as condensed a genre as poetry. Of course we are forced here to speak primarily of the translator's choice of words, as the wealth of footnotes in the modern versions bears witness.

Poetry suffers greatly in translation because it is impossible to transfer the nuances of meaning from one language to another and because the sound pattern of the original language is obviously lost when another set of sounds is substituted. But those of us who are not fluent in Hebrew can gain some appreciation of the force implied in the English words by reminding ourselves that the Hebrew words referred to things of the senses. It is fascinating to realize for example that the verb "to be jealous" was a regular form of the verb "to glow," and that "truth" derived from the verb meaning "to prop, to build, to make firm." "Self" meant also "bone." Fear was expressed by loosening of reins, despair by welling of the heart, pride by holding the head high, patience by long breathing, and impatience by short breathing. One has only to allow oneself to respond to the connotation of these examples to know immediately how accurate is the sense appeal in its counterpart definition. And we are brought straight to our modern theory of empathy which, as we already know, is the interaction of emotional and physical responses. How ridiculous, then, to try to read the poetry of the Bible with our heads alone. And what a waste not to let our voices and bodies communicate this involvement of the senses to our listeners.

The choice of words used by the translator will also affect the sound pattern of the poem. As we mentioned in Chapter Three, the effect created by the juxtaposition or close proximity of various vowels and consonants is called tone color. We are most accustomed to that aspect of tone color which we call *alliteration*, or the sameness of initial vowels or consonants at the beginning of two or more adjacent words. But tone color is a larger term and often indicates a whole pattern of similar or contrasting sounds woven through several lines of a poem. The sounds may be at the beginning of words or within them. They may be vowels or consonants or a combination of both occurring with sufficient frequency to contribute to the overall sound patterning.

The following example is from The New English Bible translation of Psalm 8. Try reading it aloud with attention to clear and full articulation of all the sounds.

> O Lord our soverign,
> how glorious is thy name in all the earth!
> Thy majesty is praised high as the heavens.
> Out of the mouths of babes, of infants at the breasts,
> thou hast rebuked the mighty,
> silencing enmity and vengeance to teach thy foes a lesson.

Notice the open *o* sounds in the first line combined with the *r* in three of the four words. The need to open the mouth for the *o* and then bring the tongue and lips and jaws to the *r* position will have an effect on pace and vocal quality. The *o/r* combination is continued in the next line in "glorious." The *a* of "name" in the second line is carried through in "praised" and "babes" in the next two lines. The open vowels and softer consonants predominate in the first five lines of praise until "rebuked," after which the tighter *i* sound combined with crisper *t*'s, the *s*'s of "mighty," "silencing," and "enmity" and the consonants of "vengeance" shift the tone. Try saying "sovereign" and "glorious" and then try "silencing enmity and vengeance" to be aware of the different jaw and tongue positions they require. Say them slowly several times being aware of their connotation, of course, and see how pace and intensity of tone adapt to the sound combinations.

Notice also the interesting sound effects of parallelism in the fulcrum lines which turn our attention to man and his unworthiness:

> what is man that thou shouldst remember him,
> mortal man that thou shouldst care for him?

If the sounds are clearly articulated they cannot be hurried. The tongue and lips and jaws will not shift that fast. The repeated "that thou," the numerous *m*'s and the *st* ending on "shouldst" all require time and precision.

Never underestimate the help that tone color provides in reading the Bible. It is partly responsible for our remembering so many of the quotations we use all our lives. The interpreter who is interested in communicating the *full* meaning of what he is reading will be sharply conscious of this sound patterning and the change it undergoes. Again let us remember that this is only one small part of the total selection and must not be allowed to distract from the whole. Rather, it underscores and intensifies the content and adds both unity and variety as well as contributing to harmony.

Parallelism

Parallelism, which we mentioned in Chapter Three, contributes strongly to tone color as well as to rhythm of thought return. Obviously any repetition of a particular word, which is basic in parallelism, repeats the sounds as well as the thought, as is clearly evident in the last example we noted. This device must be used fully and skillfully. You are responsible for whatever the translator of the version you have chosen has given you from the total organization to the smallest vowels and consonants. Trust him. There were many synonyms he could have used, and the words he chose were selected partly for their sounds. Use them.

Hebrew poetry rests on parallelism rather than on meter and rhyme. Unfortunately many of us are unable to read the original and must depend upon translators who, in most cases, have captured whatever is possible of the original not only in what it means but in how it says what it means. Sypherd defines parallelism as "a correspondence in sense and a balance in form between successive lines of a structural unit."[1] There are numerous types of parallelism but they all come under this basic definition.

Synonymous parallelism is the simplest form, wherein the thought of the first line is repeated exactly or nearly so in the second and sometimes even in the third or fourth as is true in the lines from Psalm 8 quoted above. Antithetic parallelism has the second line contrasting, often by negation, with the first, under a conforming structure. Ecclesiastes 3:1–8 is a classic example of this type of parallelism with its contrasting lines:

1. W. O. Sypherd. *The Literature of the English Bible*. (New York: Oxford University Press, 1938), p. 92.

> A time for giving birth,
> a time for dying;
> a time for planting,
> a time for uprooting what has been planted.
> (The Jerusalem Bible)

Synthetic parallelism sets up a thought in the first line and the second line completes its implication, as in

> Rich and poor are found together,
> Yahweh has made them all.
> (Prov. 22:2, The Jerusalem Bible)

Incidentally, Proverbs is particularly rich in parallelisms. Another which is found in the same Book is an inverted parallelism with the first and fourth lines corresponding and the second and third lines matching each other:

> My son, if your heart is wise,
> then my own heart is glad,
> and my inmost self rejoices
> when from your lips come honest words.
> (Prov. 23:15 and 16, The Jerusalem Bible)

There is also the "stair-like" or climactic form in which the accented words occur in progressive movement. Another is the emblematic form in which a statement in one line suggests an application in the second:

> Like bellows for the coal and fuel for the fire
> is a quarrelsome man for kindling strife.
> (Prov. 26:21, The New English Bible)

It is, of course, not necessary for the interpreter to stop and label every type of parallelism he encounters, although such a study would be fascinating one. Rather he must be aware of the rhythmic contribution parallelism makes in thought return, syntactical correspondence, and tone color.

Rhythm

As Sypherd implies in his definition of parallelism, the line in biblical poetry is important as a unit of thought and also as a unit of sound. This is true of all poetry. We mentioned in our discussion of literary style that the words grouped together in a sentence work in close relationship with one another. This concept must be expanded to include the words grouped together in a line of poetry, no matter how many lines it takes to complete a sentence. There should be a pause of some kind at the end of every line of poetry, biblical, or modern. This does *not* mean a dead stop with a terminal pause. Sometimes it is only a barely perceptible "loop pause" into the next line because the sentence as a unit must be kept intact. But we break our sentences into speech phrases even in informal conversation. We would not say the lines from Proverbs 26:21 all in one breath without a pause between "fire" and "is" for clarity and balance. Nor would we come to a full terminal pause after "fire."

A line of poetry is not only a minor thought unit but it is also a unit of the sound pattern which builds through the entire selection. Traditional English poetry scans; that is, it falls into an identical or approximate number of traditional groupings of lighter and heavier stresses per line. Those groupings are called feet and usually contain two or three syllables each with no more than two stresses. The most common English foot is probably the iamb, which is two syllables, the first being lighter than the second, and it is marked ◡ ′ . Other common feet are the anapest (◡◡ ′), the trochee (′◡), the dactyl (′◡◡), the pyrrhic (◡◡), and the spondee (′′).

Hebrew poetry, however, does not fall into these traditional groupings or feet. It finds its rhythmic base in the thought return that results from the parallelism we have discussed and in the number of heavier stresses per line regardless of their position in relation to the lighter stressed syllables. Moreover, there may be any number of lighter stressed syllables within the line. Thus, modern syllabic prosody, or the correspondence of the number of syllables per line, does not operate effectively here. Nor does foot prosody, which depends on the traditional groupings we have mentioned. Rather, the most useful prosody is stress prosody in which, as we have said, the number of heavier stresses per line establishes the rhythmic basis.

The three-stress line appears to have been the most common among the Hebrew poets. But again we are faced with the problem inherent in translations. Obviously the translators are aware of this fundamental principle of Hebrew poetry, but it is not always possible to achieve it when the language is changed into English. Also, our ears are trained to catch foot prosody more easily than stress prosody, although a large proportion of our modern poets use stress prosody extensively. The only way to discover whether your selection falls into traditional feet is to mark the lighter and heavier stresses within the lines. If there seems to be no clearly discernible pattern of traditional grouping, turn your attention to stress prosody. The important point is to find and use whatever rhythmic basis your chosen version gives you. Remember, however, that the rhythm or pulse of a line of poetry is only one of its elements and must never become so strong that it obscures the sense of what you are reading. In addition, do not try to impose an equal amount of force on all heavier stresses. They will vary in degree of intensity but will demand some stress for pronunciation or sense. Neither should you drop the lighter stressed syllables so that they disappear. Noting the lighter and heavier stresses sets up a pulse rather than a beat. Let it flow. Do not be tricked into saying

> The Lórd is my shépherd I sháll not wánt.

The verb "shall" is simply the proper future form for the first person singular and does not express determination as "will" does. Determination on the part of the *persona* would hardly be appropriate in this passage. The point of the line is, rather, I shall *not want*. Care with the tone color of "not want" will help give the line a gentle emphasis and peaceful quality. The rhythm must support the total meaning of the line, not override it.

Many inexperienced readers, having found a predominant pattern of scansion or of stresses per line, try to force every other line of the poem into strict conformity. Remember that all art contains variety and contrast within its essential unity. Do not expect every line to fall precisely into the predominant pattern. The rhythm will shift to support changes or to provide relief from monotony and allow the ear to return refreshed to the predominant pattern. Never try to push a poem into a pattern which does not exist within it by doing violence either to pronunciation or to meaning and connotation.

Let us make a graphic comparison of two versions of Psalm 8. We will study both the predominant stress pattern per line and the variety existing within that pattern. The first is from the American Revised Version of the King James translation.

Psalm 8 (American Revised Version)	*Stresses per Line*
O Jehóvah, our Lórd,	4
Hŏw éxcellĕnt ĭs thy náme ĭn all thĕ eárth,	4
Whŏ hăst sĕt thy glóry ŭpón thĕ héavĕns!	4

Psalm 8 (American Revised Version)   *Stresses*
                                                per Line

Out of the mouth of babes and sucklings hast
   thou established strength,   6
Because of thine adversaries,   4
That thou mightest still the enemy and the
   avenger.   4
When I consider thy heavens, the work of thy
   fingers,   5
The moon and the stars, which thou hast ordained;   4
What is man, that thou art mindful of him?   5
And the son of man, that thou visitest him?   5
For thou hast made him but little lower than God,   4
And crownest him with glory and honor.   4
Thou makest him to have dominion over the works
   of thy hands;   5
Thou hast put all things under his feet: 5
All sheep and oxen,   3
Yea, and the beasts of the field,   3
The birds of the heavens, and the fish of the sea,   4
Whatsoever passeth through the paths of the seas.   5
O Jehovah, our Lord,   4
How excellent is thy name in all the earth!   4

Obviously the lines differ widely in length so it is apparent that our structural unity does not come from conformity of sound flow either within lines or speech phrases.
Only six of the twenty lines are completely regular in the
use of iambic and anapestic feet so we will discard the
theory of foot prosody and look at the number of stresses
per line. More than half of the lines have four stresses
each. This basis is established with the opening lines and
returned to at fairly regular intervals throughout the selec-

tion. Against this basic four-stress line there is a counter-rhythm provided by the five-stress lines which first appear in line 7 and alternate in pairs with the four-stress lines in the middle of the poem, appearing again just before the final couplet.

The Jerusalem Bible translation is somewhat less patterned in its stresses per line. There is a very slight predominance of four-stress lines but hardly enough to offer overwhelming evidence that its undeniable pulse comes from that source. So we must look further. Many of the lines fall into a fairly regular scansion pattern of iambs and anapests but again there is probably more variety than conformity. Examining the way the lines divide into speech phrases in order to take full advantage of the tone color and imagery, as well as the condensed balance of such lines as "by the mouths of children, babes in arms," we find that the following pattern emerges. The speech phrases are separated by slashes.

Psalm 8 (The Jerusalem Bible)	Stresses per Line	Stresses per Speech Phrase
Yáhwĕh, / oúr Lórd,	3	1–2
hŏw gréat yoŭr náme / throŭghoút thĕ eárth!	4	2–2
Abóvĕ thĕ heávĕns / iš yoŭr májĕstў chántĕd	4	2–2
bў thĕ moúths ŏf chíldrĕn, / bábes ĭn árms.	4	2–2
Yoŭ sét yoŭr strónghŏld / fírm / agaínst yoŭr foés	5	2–1–2
Tŏ sŭbdúe énĕmiĕs / ănd rébĕls.	3	2–1
Ĭ loók úp ăt yoŭr heávĕns, / máde bў yoŭr fíngĕrs,	5	3–2

Psalm 8 (The Jerusalem Bible)

	Stresses per Line	Stresses per Speech Phrase
at the moon and stars / you set in place —	5	2–3
ah, / what is man / that you should spare a thought / for him,	7	1–2–3–1
the son of man / that you should care for him?	5	2–3
Yet / you have made him little less than a god,	5	1–4
you have crowned him with glory / and splendour,	3	2–1
made him lord / over the work of your hands,	5	2–3
set all things / under his feet,	5	3–2
sheep and oxen, / all these,	4	2–2
yes, / wild animals too,	4	1–3
birds in the air, / fish in the sea	4	2–2
travelling the paths of the ocean.	3	3
Yahweh, our Lord,	3	1–2
how great your name / throughout the earth!	4	2–2

The predominance of the two-stress speech phrase is immediately apparent. All but three lines contain at least one. There is a preponderance of masculine endings varied by at least one feminine ending in each stanza.

Thus far we have been looking for elements of rhythmic unity. But sometimes this rhythmic unity is so strong that it becomes a problem and we must look for every detail which will help us control it. One of the most difficult passages in the Bible is the familiar passage from Ecclesiastes (3:1–8) in which there is a tremendous danger of monotony and of the clearly evident rhythmic basis becoming so strong that it obscures not only meaning but emotive content as well. The King James version does not arrange the lines in poetic format, but it is so highly rhythmic that the method of analysis we will suggest for the two following modern translations is clearly applicable to The King James version as well.

We mentioned these verses earlier as a classic example of antithetic parallelism. It is in the *precise* rhythmic quality that most of the problems are centered when this material is read aloud by the unwary. Since the typography of The New English Bible and The Jerusalem Bible differ, we will refer at the moment to verses rather than lines. The word choice differs somewhat also, but the essential organization of thought is, of course, identical. The chapter opens with the prose line, "There is a season for everything, a time for every occupation under heaven" in The Jerusalem Bible, and with the line, "For everything its season, and for every activity under heaven its time" in The New English Bible. The reader is then immediately confronted with absolutely parallel syntax for twenty-seven lines beginning "a time for" with one single variation of "a time to" in The Jerusalem Bible, and with fourteen lines containing "a time to . . . and a time to [or for]" in The New English Bible. Certainly there is no lack of unity and pattern! Of course the antithesis inherent in the parallelism will provide contrast but even so the pattern is so strong as to require careful control.

Realizing the organization of thought progression will help to bring about this control. Notice that verses 2 and 3 are both concerned with creating and destroying, with creating coming first in "birth . . . dying" and "planting. . . uprooting." The order is reversed, however, in verse 3, as "killing" precedes "healing" and "knocking down" precedes "building." Verse 4 turns to a consideration of joy and sorrow with "tears," "laughter," "mourning," and "dancing." Verses 5 and 6 deal with keeping and losing or throwing away. Even verse 7 echoes the foregoing themes with "tearing and sewing," which imply destroying and then rescuing. This is followed by "silence" and "speaking," and we then move into the reversed unit of "love," "hate," "war," and "peace." Attention to this aspect of organization will allow the interpreter to group the related "times" and to set them off as units by minor pauses and slight changes in inflection pattern.

But even such grouping will not completely solve the problem of the strong patterning. Let us look at the two translations, marking the lighter and heavier stresses, and try to discover some helpful variations. We will number the lines for easier reference.

The Jerusalem Bible version reads as follows:

1 A time for giving birth,
2 a time for dying;
3 a time for planting,
4 a time for uprooting what has been planted.
5 A time for killing,
6 a time for healing;
7 a time for knocking down,
8 a time for building.
9 A time for tears,
10 a time for laughter;
11 a time for mourning,
12 a time for dancing.
13 A time for throwing stones away,
14 a time for gathering them up;
15 a time for embracing,
16 a time to refrain from embracing.

17 A time for searching,
18 a time for losing;
19 a time for keeping,
20 a time for throwing away.
21 A time for tearing,
22 a time for sewing;
23 a time for keeping silent,
24 a time for speaking.
25 A time for loving,
26 a time for hating;
27 a time for war,
28 a time for peace.

The New English Bible differs in its use of the infinitive in all but two lines, instead of the participial form of the verbs used in the Jerusalem, and it places the two elements of the parallelism on the same line. The spacing below will make the pattern more graphic:

1 a time to be born   and a time to die;
2 a time to plant   and a time to uproot;
3 a time to kill   and a time to heal;
4 a time to pull down   and a time to build up;
5 a time to weep   and a time to laugh;
6 a time for mourning   and a time for dancing;
7 a time to scatter stones   and a time to gather them;
8 a time to embrace   and a time to refrain from
                                   embracing;
9 a time to seek   and a time to lose;
10 a time to keep   and a time to throw away;
11 a time to tear   and a time to mend;
12 a time for silence   and a time for speech;
13 a time to love   and a time to hate;
14 a time for war   and a time for peace.

The structure of both versions is basically regular, as is to be expected with such strict parallelism. Both fall easily into a predominantly iambic-anapestic meter. But there are some small details that add variety within this structure, as will be apparent from the tables below. We will not be concerned with speech phrases in The Jerusalem Bible version because the lines are much too brief to break. We will consider only the line length counts. The New English Bible version, however, demands a pause within its lines to set off the opposing member of the antithesis, so in the right-hand columns we will ignore line lengths and include the speech phrase counts.

Rhythmic details, Ecclesiastes 3:1–8

The Jerusalem Bible		*The New English Bible*		
Syllables per Line	*Stresses per Line*	*Stresses per Line*	*Syllables per Speech Phrase*	*Stresses per Speech Phrase*
6	3	4	5–5	2–2
5	2	4	4–6	2–2
5	2	4	4–5	2–2
11	3	6	5–6	3–3
5	2	4	4–5	2–2
5	2	4	5–6	2–2
6	3	6	6–7	3–3
5	2	5	5–10	2–3
4	2	4	4–5	2–2
5	2	5	4–7	2–3
5	2	4	4–5	2–2
5	2	4	5–5	2–2
8	4	4	4–5	2–2
8	3	4	4–5	2–2
6	2			
9	3			

Syllables per Line	Stresses per Line	Stresses per Line	Syllables per Speech Phrase	Stresses per Speech Phrase
5	2			
5	2			
5	2			
7	3			
5	2			
5	2			
7	3			
5	2			
5	2			
5	2			
4	2			
4	2			

In The Jerusalem Bible the majority of the lines have five syllables and two stresses, but there are also lines with from four to eleven syllables, and at no time are there more than three five-syllable lines in succession. Within the predominance of two stresses per line, there are seven with three stresses and one with four stresses. They are scattered throughout the verses and never appear in succession. Although this translation uses mostly feminine endings, due in part to the participial verb forms, eight of the lines have masculine endings which adds another element of much needed variety when the verses are read aloud.

In The New English Bible version, the three feminine line-endings provide variety against the predominance of masculine endings. In addition, two of the speech phrases (lines 6 and 12) end on lighter stresses within the lines. The prevalence of five-syllable speech phrases is not as strong here as that provided by the five-syllable lines in The Jerusalem Bible, and in only two lines (1 and 12) are the speech phrases of equal length. The prominence of the two-stress speech phrase is tempered by the insertion of occasional three-stress speech phrases, three of which occur in the lines with the feminine endings.

These details may seem to be inconsequential in themselves but when taken together with the variation in tone color and the various aspects of organization and grouping, they help to achieve the variety that is so important in preventing monotony and assuring that the verses are interpreted in a meaningful and moving way.

At this point, or perhaps well before this, a question and a protest have probably entered your mind. The question may well be, "Did the writer, or translator, know he was doing all this?" That, of course, is impossible to answer, but whether or not he was conscious of it, it is there for us to work with. Anyone who knows the Psalms is aware that many of them are carefully and skillfully wrought, the acrostic structuring of Psalm 111 and the alphabetical organization of Psalms 119 and 145, for instance. These elements are largely lost in translation but clearly indicate that the Psalms were not, for the most part, undisciplined bursts by unskilled singers. Any translator who would undertake the monumental task of putting such poetry into another language would certainly be aware of all the technical aspects of the original and would take care to preserve everything possible in the transference of languages.

The protest is a great deal simpler to answer. If you are saying to yourself, "Do you mean to say I have to do all that marking and digging before I can read the Bible aloud?" the answer is, "No, not if you are content merely to read the words and communicate only the gist of the message." But if you wish to do justice to the literature, then you must be willing to find everything that is in it and use it to communicate the totality of your selection. Obviously, after you have looked in detail at a few selections, the process will become easier because you know where to look for what you need to find. Soon there will only be a few really difficult passages that you will need to chart. Your ear will be attuned to the sources of rhythm, and your awareness of imagery, tone color, and shifts of thought and attitude within the organization of the selection will help you achieve both the unity and the variety within it. What we have covered in analysis will be applicable to all the biblical poetry you undertake to read but, of course, the results will vary with each individual selection. Find what is there and then decide how to use your own techniques to make full use of it.

9

Lamentations

In the preceding chapter our attention was focused on brief poetic units. Since we have already studied an extended narrative unit of prose it might be of some interest to examine an extended poetic unit as well. All the stylistic aspects which were touched on in our discussion of Psalms and Proverbs must also be considered here.

Lamentations, the extended unit of poetry we shall be looking at, combines many of the elements we have discussed in both poetry and prose, in terms of organization, climaxes, persona, and other matters. Lamentations is a somewhat neglected book in modern Bible reading, due in part to its length, but it would make a fine contribution to special Bible services and it reads beautifully. All the quotations will be taken from the excellent translation by Delbert R. Hillers in The Anchor Bible.[1]

Lamentations is a difficult book to classify. Some versions place it with the prophetic writings while some, notably the Hebrew, do not. It has units of narrative but must be considered basically lyric. It has been called a

1. The Anchor Bible (New York: Doubleday, 1967), vol. 7a.

dirge and the three-two succession of stresses per line in the Hebrew bears out this category. But that is too general a statement, in view of all its variety. There are indeed passages of mourning, resignation, and patient endurance, but there is also a strong undertone of the tenacity of the Jewish character; and its overall message is an expression of hope and faith that God's mercy has not come to an end. A nation is called to penance but there is an underlying confidence that mercy will eventually be forthcoming although it will not be quick or easy to obtain.

History is no longer a basis of hope for the persona or personae of Lamentations. Indeed, the fact that the Jews have sinned so deeply and come to such a tragic pass marks the end of the traditional belief that they were considered Yahweh's chosen people. As Hillers in his excellent Introduction to his translation says:

> . . . the Book of Kings states the facts about the fall of Jerusalem in 587 B.C. Lamentations supplies the meaning of the facts. It is first of all a recital of the horrors and atrocities that came during the long siege and its aftermath, but beyond the tale of physical sufferings it tells of the spiritual significance of the fall of the city.

Lamentations was originally thought to be the work of Jeremiah and is sometimes so titled. Many modern scholars, however, discount this theory. Whoever wrote the Book, whether it be one man or several, was certainly a poet who knew his craft and how to control it. The five poems are remarkable in the sophistication of their structure. Each is shaped by the Hebrew alphabet. We touched on this influence of sound on Hebrew prosody when we discussed the Psalms and noted the impossibility of realizing it fully in translation. But the fact that it exists in the original language is proof that the poet knew what he was doing and signals the interpreter to look carefully at all the details he finds even in the translations. Hillers' version preserves some of this alphabetical precision, especially in the third poem, although of course an exact sequence would be impossible. His discussion in the Introduction, "Notes and Comments," is particularly interesting and informative.

The entire book of Lamentations is built on a metaphor or perhaps more properly a personification of the people of Judah, and by analogy, of the city itself as a woman. She is the "Daughter of Zion" with the "of" being in apposition rather than operating as possessive, so that she is both Zion and the people of Zion.

Poem I

The first poem (1:1–22) is probably the most formal of the five and the most purely a dirge. It opens with "How" or with "Oh, how" in The Jerusalem Bible, as do the second and fourth poems. This is traditional and serves as the title for the entire book in The Hebrew Bible; it is an exclamation rather than a question, as the punctuation indicates. The persona is third person as the poem begins, and he recounts the horrors and desolation of Judah, using always the personification we mentioned above. The account reaches a climax of pathos with the lines

All her people are groaning, seeking food.
They gave their darlings for food, to keep alive (1:11).

At this point the persona changes to first person, and the prayer of anguish which follows is obviously spoken by the woman. We have had a forewarning of this change in the last line of verse 9 where we find " 'Yahweh, look upon my misery, at the insolence of the enemy!' " Hillers' translation puts the woman's speeches in quotation marks, while The New English Bible makes use of the third person with

> Look, Lord, upon her misery,
> see how the enemy has triumphed (1:9).

We wish to make no comment on authenticity here but merely to point out that the interpreter must be very sure he knows who is speaking what lines. There is another line just before the climax of pathos which Hillers also handles as a direct quotation, but it is a recording of an edict, "They shall not enter your assembly" (1:10), rather than an immediate statement from God; this statement probably need not have a strong degree of characterization but should be treated more as something which has been passed down through many generations.

The first person persona continues her lament until verse 17, where there is again an insertion of the third person but only for a single verse. It is here that the tone shifts somewhat from a mere accounting to

> Yahweh is in the right, for I disobeyed his command.
> Listen, all you peoples, and realize my pain!

This first poem is almost overwhelming in its kinetic and kinesthetic imagery, and the demands for empathy are undeniable. It is strangely sparse in the visual and auditory imagery which is usually so much a part of prophetic writings, except for the references to emptiness and desolation in which the sights are not important in themselves but rather for the physical responses which they evoke.

Surprisingly, it is not rich in similes and metaphors. The only two similes it contains carry strong physical implications. The first is "Jerusalem has become like an unclean thing in their midst" followed by the much more fully developed and powerful

> Her princes were like stags which could find no pasture,
> But went on exhausted before the hunter (1:6).

The three metaphors which exist within the extended metaphor of the whole poem occur in verses 13, 14 and 15. They have to do with a net for the feet, entangled steps, and a yoke on the neck, and the remarkable line "The Lord trod the wine-press of fair young Judah" (1:15). A great number of strong figures of speech would no doubt have distracted from the metaphorical function of the personification on which the poem is based.

There are spots of remarkable tone color in the version we are discussing, such as "By night she weeps aloud, tears on her cheeks" (1:2), where the long *e* sounds and the open vowels of "aloud" emphasize the connotation. There are not many such lines, but where they occur they heighten the pathos and give needed variety to the heavy rhythm set by coincidence of line lengths and sentence lengths. Every line but two has some punctuation at its termination and most of them end in periods. This can threaten variety and must be tempered by the uneven division of the line into speech phrases and by every device available to keep the poem from "coming out in slices." Connotation, of course, will help vary pace, and the number of feminine line-ends will also be useful.

Poems, II, III, IV, V

Structurally, poems II and IV are similar to I, using as they do the alphabetical sequence, but poem IV uses two-line stanzas rather than the three-line stanza found in I and II. There is considerable difference, also, in the handling of content. Poem II is again a recounting of miseries, but the focus here is on the Lord's enmity. There are many battle motifs and such verbs as "thrown down (the glory of Israel)," "consumed," "tore down," "brought down to earth," "lopped off (the horns of Israel)," "bent (his bow)," to mention a few. These abound in the first eight verses and are spoken by a third person narrator. The continuing use of the past tense in contrast to the present tense which predominates in poem I adds a degree of distancing and also hints at the length of time that God has been "like an enemy." In verse 9 there is a change to the present tense, with present and past alternating, although not perfectly, throughout the rest of the poem.

The first person singular pronoun first occurs in verses 11 and 12. Hillers does not put them in quotation marks, indicating that he considers them still part of the third person persona's speech. This seems quite acceptable in light of the poet's involvement in the grief over the fate of the city and the people. However it might be equally feasible to consider them as an insertion of a commentary by the personified Zion. Verse 13, however, which continues with the first person, is clearly not the woman, for the poet says, "What likeness can I use to comfort you, O fair Zion?" Thus probably the unity is better served by following Hillers' decision. There are a few examples of direct address in the comments and taunts of Zion's enemies, but she herself does not speak in her own person until after the exhortation for prayer in verses 18 and 19. Verses 20–22 might even be attributed to the third person/first person poet-persona, except for the last line, "My enemies have wiped out those whom I cherished and brought up," which refers back directly to the admonition in verse 19: "Lift up your hands to him for the lives of your children."

This poem is much richer in metaphors and similes than the first one, lacking as it does the metaphorical strength of consistent personification. There are motifs of fire, penance, and silence. The images are strongly physical and include appeals to almost every one of the senses. There is a heavy downward pull to the entire poem, balanced by the intensity of Yahweh's actions. It does not even have the slight rise of pace which comes from submission and admission of guilt which is found in the prayer that closes the first poem.

Poem III uses the alphabetical structuring for its three-line stanzas with the same letter beginning each line of a stanza. This strict structure, which also tightens the stanza divisions, is relieved somewhat by the speech phrase divisions within the lines, which also help vary the coincidence of sentence, and line length, which we mentioned in the other poems. Here every single line has some sort of end punctuation, and again the majority of them are periods and there are fewer feminine endings. The interpreter must take great care to keep a flow to the thought progression. He will find some help in the fact that in several of the stanzas there is a turn of thought in the middle line that is then developed or at least carried over into the following stanza.

The problem of persona is a difficult one in this poem. He is probably comparable to the "Survivor" in Poem IV. and is, as Hillers suggests, a sort of Everyman. It is he who writes the note of hope in verses 22 through 24 with the lines

> Yahweh's mercy is surely not at an end, nor is his pity exhausted.
> It is new every morning. Great is your faithfulness!
> Yahweh is my portion, I tell myself, therefore I will hope.

As a matter of fact, these lines act as the fulcrum for

the entire Book although there are frequent extended returns to the mourning. Immediately after the above lines, there is a subtle shift away from the specific "I" to "the person," and "a man," with the exact center of the poem moving toward a widening of focus which leads to the inclusive "Let us" exhortation to penance and prayer in verses 40 and 41. There is a return to the first person singular with verse 48, but the "I" has become more collective than it was at the opening.

The fourth section Hillers entitles "A Survivor's Account." Again there are references to "my people," but the speaker is clearly not Zion but one who is an eyewitness to the fate of the people in the city in contrast to their past, as seen in

> Those who once fed on delicacies are destitute in the
> streets;
> Those brought up in scarlet clothing pick through
> garbage (4.5).

and again in

> Her Nazarites were whiter than snow, lighter than milk.
> Their bodies were more ruddy than corals; their beards
> were lapis lazuli.
> Now they look blacker than soot; they are not recognized
> in the street.
> Their skin has shrunk over their bones, has become dry
> as wood (4:7-8).

The account of the fall of the city and the flight into the desert ends with the poignant verse 20:

> The breath of our nostrils, the annointed of Yahweh, was
> caught in their traps,
> The one of whom we said "In his shadow we will live
> among the nations."

The last two verses are concerned with a warning that is actually a curse directed against Edom. It will be remembered that it was the people of Edom who would not permit the children of Israel to cross their land in their exile, thus forcing them to take the long way around and add many months to their journey (Nos. 20). But Zion's punishment is complete and Yahweh will not exile her again.

Poem V is a simple and moving prayer and the persona is clear. All the references are to "us" and "our." There is a steady rhythm of balance between "you" (Yahweh) and "us" who suffer from the fathers' sins. This is contrasted with the center section (5:8-13) with its references to "they" as the rulers. It is particularly rich in parallelisms and again will require careful control to make it effective and bring the book to the quiet, penitent, and almost childlike close: "You have been very angry with us" (5:22).

Lamentations is a challenge to the interpreter, but with close analysis it can become one of the most exciting of the books of the Old Testament. It is a remarkable piece of poetic achievement and a moving documentary of suffering and patience, hope and faith. It must be carefully analyzed as to content and structure. It requires skill and dedication on the part of the interpreter to fully communicate both its note of heavy mourning, which sometimes tolls like a great bell through the deliberately patterned lines, and the qualities of endurance and submission that will lead Zion to peace and absolution.

10
Prophecies and Revelations

The prophetic writings of the Old Testament and the revelations in the New Testament have many qualities in common. Most of them are a blend of several types of literature and have in common a first person speaker or persona. This last characteristic they share, of course, with the Epistles; and, like the Epistles, they were addressed to specific situations—quite probably specific groups in assembly.

When we speak of prophetic *writings,* however, we are not using the term *writing* in the modern sense. Undoubtedly almost all of the prophecies were delivered orally and written down much later, either from memory or from scattered notes. They are not addressed to a single person but rather are intended for the entire nation of Israel. The purpose was to keep the Israelites faithful to the true religion of Yahweh, in which respect they fulfill the same function as the Epistles. But in contrast to the Epistles, the prophecies, although revealed through visions of divine inspiration, included highly graphic and specific descriptions of the consequences of infidelity to or transgression against the law of Yahweh. This is consistent with the ancient Hebrew concept of reward or punishment in this world rather than in the life to come. The recounting of visions is highly charged with emotion and appeals to all the senses. The speaker has witnessed the scenes and heard the discourse which he is under compulsion to share with his listeners. The accounts are episodic and their allusions are strongly metaphorical. There is a preponderance of poetry within them which heightens their emotive content. They require a willingness to let them operate on this high emotional level which, of course, involves the interpreter's voice and body response as well as his understanding of the part they played in the history of Israel.

At about the middle of the eighth century B.C. the long tradition of prophecy and inspired "mouthpieces of God" underwent a distinct change. The whole cult or profession had fallen from the high position it formerly held, due to some extent to the number of charlatans who found it lucrative. But with the advent of Amos and Hosea in the north and Isaiah and Micah in the south there began what is commonly called the classic period of prophecy, and the words of these four and those who followed them are preserved for us in their separate books.

Any attempt to place them chronologically, however, immediately plunges one into difficulty because scholars agree that the prophetic books, probably more than most of the other biblical writings, have been edited and amended, added to and condensed or expanded by numerous writers throughout the centuries. Likewise it is impossible to make up an exclusive list of prophetic sections that covers all the Old Testament references and satisfies all readers, since the Jewish, Catholic, and Protestant Bibles differ slightly in categorization. Our concern here, then, will be with the general characteristics of prophetic writing as they affect the interpreter's task of communicating with his listeners. We will make specific references from time to time to the so-called major prophets and to "The Twelve" who are sometimes referred to as the minor prophets or, in The Hebrew Bible, as Later Prophets.

Literary style within the prophecies varies widely and it will be necessary to keep in mind all we have said about style analysis of narratives and poetry in the Bible. But whether the writing be poetry, narrative, didactic prose, or something closely related to dramatic discourse, the prophecies by their very nature present a unique problem to the interpreter.

The Prophecies

The prophets in the Old Testament cannot be classified as "ecstatic" prophets who spoke from a seizure or a trance-like state. Neither were they foretellers of the future. Certainly there is much foretelling in their messages but that was not their primary function. The predicting of future events was always done to make a point in the present. In any case, their utterances were drawn from the depth of their beings. They spoke as men who had been called to a divine and often difficult vocation. Several of them tell us of their being summoned and some, Amos (5:8) and Jeremiah (20:7-10), for example, admit their reluctance to accept the calling. Jonah, of course, got on a ship and fled the Lord!

The prophetic writings have been referred to as an anthology or even an anthology of anthologies, and the interpreter will not find in them even the degree of unity discernible in the Epistles. There is no clearly developed chronological progression from one section to another. Often the only clue to unity is the intensity of the speaker about the matters at hand.

Time, place, and historical circumstances are basic in any consideration of the prophetic writings. The allusions, often difficult for a modern audience, are drawn from the objects, people, places, and events which will most quickly and dramatically highlight what the speaker knows is in the minds of the addressees: their wars, their desolations, their social problems, and their hope for Yahweh's intervention in their behalf.

Although we have mentioned the difficulty of placing the writings in exact chronological order, it is important to keep in mind the *approximate* time, place, and historical circumstances that gave rise to these tracts. The words of Amos were spoken in a time of great wealth and luxury for Israel. The rich lived for their own pleasure and were corrupt, effete, and vicious in their dealings with their fellow men. Amos spoke out against their hedonism and called for social justice and a return to some of the old simplicities.

His style is vivid with imagery and direct in its syntax. He begins nearly every stanza or unit with "These are the words of the Lord" or "This is what the Lord showed me." There are no sections in which he speaks of himself or his own justification for speaking, but rather he offers short admonitions such as "Listen, Israelites," and then moves directly into what was seen or said, using a colon instead of starting a new sentence. The dialogue in the prose section (chapters 7 and 8) is direct, strong, and dramatic. The poetry is full of highly emotive words, with a particularly telling repetition in the section on the sins of Israel and her neighbors, where eight stanzas open with the name of a different criminal inserted in the first line

> For the crime after crime of . . .
> I will grant them no reprieve because . . .
> > (1:3–2:7, The New English Bible)

Stresses are clustered together for force and emphasis in the poetry, and the speech phrases usually coincide with the line length; the majority of lines end on a stress.

Hosea, speaking at the same time and in the same general area, has been called the prophet of pity. He was a man of some substance, as was Amos, and there is a strong undercurrent of personal experience in his allusions and metaphors. He cites the imperative duty of love, which is certainly not unrelated to Amos's pleas for justice. But Hosea uses appeals to the more tender emotions. His analogy of Israel's relationship with God to that of a wife with her husband is particularly apt as he develops it. His style, perhaps as a result of his emotional bent, is often a series of extracts having topical unity but featuring rapid transitions from denunciations to passionate pleas and sometimes exclamations at the climactic moment. There are flashes of brilliant and vivid imagery and dramatic figures of speech such as

> That is why I am going to block her way with thorns,
> and wall her in so she cannot find her way; (2:8–9)

and later in the same chapter:

> I will break bow, sword and battle in the country,
> and make her sleep secure (2:18).

It is interesting to contrast two brief sections on the decline of religion and simple worship in Israel. The first is from Amos and the second is from Hosea as they are translated in The Jerusalem Bible.

> I hate and despise your feasts,
> I take no pleasure in your solemn festivals. . . .
> Let me have no more of the din of your chanting,
> no more of your strumming on harps.
>   (Amos 5:21 and 23)

> Wine, new wine addles the wits.
> My people consult their block of wood,
> a rod answers their questions;
> (Hos. 4:12)

In Judah the prophet Micah cried out in grief and anxiety at the fall and dissolution of the kingdom of the north. He was a native of Moresheth and was suspicious of city life and the complexities of trade and the urban economy as is evident from 6:9–14, again using The Jerusalem Bible version:

> The voice of Yahweh. He is calling to the city:
> Listen, tribe, and assembly of the city
> whose rich men are crammed with violence,
> whose citizens are liars.
> Must I put up with fraudulent measure,
> or that abomination the short-weight bushel?
> Must I hold the man honest who measures with false
> scales and a bag of faked weights?

Chapter 6 is considered a classic among all the vivid and varied writings of the prophetic books with its trial before the mountains which begin with

> Stand up and let the case begin in the hearing of the mountains and let the hills hear what you say (6:1).

The book of Micah is entirely in poetry in most modern versions and there is a great versatility in the structure of the various units.

Isaiah, who was prominent in his country's affairs and was probably a national figure, conceived of his mission as the proclamation of the fall of Israel and of Judah and the punishment of the nation's infidelity. The second part of his book is widely believed to be the work of another and to fall roughly into the period of exile. This could certainly account for the change from the threatening oracles to what is sometimes called the "Book of the Consolation of

Israel" with its four lyrical passages of the "Songs of the Servant of Yahweh" (42:1–5, 49:4–9, 52:13 and 53:12). There is also a change in style from the energetic and imaginative figures of speech and vivid visual imagery of the first section to the repetitive and rhetorical style of the later chapters.

It is difficult to resist the temptation to treat exhaustively each of the prophets separately in terms of his organization, syntax, and other stylistic elements, because each presents his own individual peculiarities. Yet some strong similarities do exist. Jeremiah and Ezekiel, for instance, with the former's interest in the place of the individual in religion and the latter's belief in the individual's responsibility for good and evil, seem very close to each other philosophically. They do differ widely in style, however, although they were of the same era. Jeremiah was genuinely concerned over the sins of his people and pleaded with them in highly emotional terms. Ezekiel, on the other hand, uses a formal style reflecting perhaps his training and position as a high churchman.

Technically, of course, Moses was probably the greatest of the prophets and the most important in the history of the nation, for God appeared to him directly innumerable times. Indeed, all of Leviticus and most of Numbers report God's many conversations with Moses, as he gave him the Laws, instructed him in the ritual of worship even to the arrangement of candles in the standards, directed him on a journey, and educated him in the taking of the census and numerous other practical and spiritual matters. The reports of these encounters differ in many ways, however, from the works we have discussed previously, one of the most important being the absence of first person narrator. The Books of Joshua, Judges, Samuel, and Kings are often classified as primarily prophetic works. The Hebrew Bible groups them together as "The Early Prophets" as, of course, they are. But the narrator or recorder operates primarily as a third person reporter and for our purposes this does not present the same problem as the first person speaker in the books we have been considering. This is also true of most of Daniel, although the visions are delivered in the first person and thus come closer to what we have been discussing.

In all the prophetic writings, the transitions are rapid and exclamations are frequent. The climaxes are reached quickly. There is often no denouement at all within a section, or it turns suddenly from the event to the prophet's own person and actions, as is true in many of the visions. The lesson is always for the present although the events recounted are past, or sometimes future, and sometimes so highly dramatized as to be of another world entirely.

These factors present a problem of balance for the interpreter, who must make the climaxes and visions and autobiographical insertions as intense as were the experiences which evoked them, and yet be alert for the instantaneous shift to the "lesson for today." There is a constant balancing of threat (and usually a very specific one of physical involvement) and consolation, and pardon and punishment are complementary rather than a matter of cause and effect. God's will is primary and the prophet speaks of it without explanation or rationalization.

The prophets' compulsion to speak gives the prophecies an intensity which the interpreter must not ignore. The prophets did not waste time with long introductions. They, like most of the speakers in the Bible and especially in the Old Testament, took immediate command and related at once whose attention was demanded by Yahweh. They spoke from an immediate experience with God, and the happenings and conversations are reported directly (and often in direct discourse rather than indirect discourse), thus heightening the immediacy of the reported experience. Yahweh speaks in his own person through the prophet, and the words are his.

It will be helpful here to recall our discussion of the degree of the characterization of God within the narratives of both the Old and the New Testaments.

The prophets were convinced that they had been called as mouthpieces of the Lord. They did not speak for themselves, but rather God spoke through them, and they were able to see the future as well as the past and present through God's eyes. They were a unique phenomenon and although a modern audience may have difficulty accepting their utterances as factual they were nevertheless an important part of the history of Israel and first-rate "spellbinders." The clues to their effectiveness are clearly in the writing, whatever is decided about their authenticity. They must not be made to suffer from scholarly commentary and footnotes during the process of sharing their prophecies with the listeners. The prophecies stand as they are and must be so communicated.

The importance of the visions must not be underestimated. They are filled with action which the interpreter's body and voice must reflect. It is believed that the prophets often acted out what God said he would do, or what they saw in the visions. This is not to suggest that the interpreter actually break a water jar, but that he pay careful attention to all the kinetic and kinesthetic imagery that is so vital to the selections.

All types of sense imagery are found in the visions and, indeed, in every sentence of the writings. Sense imagery must be responded to fully by the interpreter to allow the audience to share in the heightened experience he is relating. The style is oracular and all our physical senses are bombarded. The interpreter need not fear he will be overly dramatic with these visions if he remains absolutely true to the writing. It is only when he himself interferes by adding his own comment, either on the writing or on his own abilities, that the effect can become too dramatic. God spoke through the prophets and they speak through whomever chooses to read them aloud. The speaker and point of view are clearly defined and basic to their effectiveness.

Another problem which may confront us in trying to read a long section from the books of the prophets involves the frequent changing from first to third person without warning. This intrigues and troubles scholars who attempt to evaluate and define authorship, but it presents the interpreter with quite another dilemma. It is clear what kind of person is speaking when the prophet uses the first person. It is either Yahweh, or the prophet answering Yahweh, or a character of some dimension within the visions, such as the cup-bearer-in-chief who "stood erect, and shouted loudly" in Isaiah 36. We are often given such "stage directions" and must use them within the bounds of good taste.

Yahweh speaks as a great, all-powerful, merciful but just God. He rules the universe and is omnipotent. Nevertheless he deigns to speak directly to a chosen one of his people on matters of great importance. The chosen prophet would certainly be filled with awe at this, but it must be remembered that the appearance of God, either in his own form or as an object, was not unheard of in the Old Testament. Therefore, the prophet would not flee or cringe in terror but rather would accept the visitation as a matter of great portent and communicate it faithfully to his listeners.

When the style switches suddenly to third person and a narrator takes over we may assume someone else is reporting what was seen and heard. But he is not an objective narrator. He, too, feels compelled to share what he knows with his listeners. Therefore, he reports with great intensity, whether in first or third person. The immediacy is only slightly lessened, if at all, in the latter case.

The Book of Revelation

The Book of Revelation is basically narrative in structure, describing as it does a chronologically arranged series of events. Nevertheless it seems wise to treat it in this chapter in relation to the prophetic writings because of the many characteristics the two have in common; this despite the fact that the prophets *heard* the word of God and passed it on *orally* while the author or authors of Revelation received a *vision* and passed it on in *writing*. Obviously there will be differences in organization and possibly in other aspects of style, but Revelation, like the books of prophecy, is a tract for its time and grew out of a specific set of circumstances and a particular time of disturbance and bitter persecution in the history of the church.

Ezekiel, with his vivid use of form and color, and Zechariah and his visions of animals and strange beasts, come immediately to mind as one reads the Book of Revelation. These two Old Testament prophets probably were the strongest influence in the establishment of the apocalyptic tradition, which was already in full force by Daniel's time.

The exact date of composition of Revelation, like the precise identity of John, is a matter of debate among scholars. Most modern critics now believe that the John of Revelation was not the same as John the apostle. As we mentioned earlier, this type of concern is not a primary one for our purposes. The date is placed somewhere between 70 and 95 A.D. and the state of Rome's relationship to the newly established church remained, unfortunately, fairly constant during those years.

The organization of ideas and their development is not as clear and precise in Revelation as that found in some of John the apostle's writing. There are breaks in the sequence which cause some scholars to think that it was compiled from several sources, or that chapters have been lost or, according to a recent theory, that there are actually two separate apocalypses written by the same author at different times and later fused into one, either by the original author or by another. In any case, the book works very well as a unit when it is read aloud within the context of a vision which need not, one supposes, follow a realistic and orderly sequence of events. John is most careful to indicate a shift in episode and we encounter frequent phrases such as "Now in my vision," "Next I saw," "Then," and "What I saw next." The interpreter need only use these to plunge at once into another episode within the framework of the vision, being careful to have concluded the episode which precedes it.

The Book begins as an Epistle with the usual salutation following the prologue of testimony of John's having been called to prophesy. This is followed by a brief account of the beginning of the vision. Each of the seven letters to the seven churches begins with the same admonition that has been given to John by the "figure like a Son of man" and they all end with the warning, "If anyone has ears to hear, let him listen to what the Spirit is saying to the churches"; there is some slight variation in the rest of the concluding sentences of the first three letters.

Since these letters are so short, they have no real organizational problems. Although the time and circumstances of the letters must be borne in mind, they are not primarily historical documents but are, like the prophecies, tracts recorded under particular circumstances for a particular audience. The infant Church was being beset by disturbance and persecution, and the Revelation which John reports is an epic of hope and something of a song of future victory based on God's promise to be with his people—a promise made in Exodus and repeated by Jesus in Matthew.

The writing is rich in symbolism and cannot, of course, be taken on a literal level. The symbolism makes for certain difficulties in comprehension, but on the whole John is careful to explain such important things as the mysticism of the number seven and the meaning of some of the animals and other elements found in his vision. The letters reflect the same intensity of experience as that found in the prophecies; the writer is clearly reporting an awesome and exhilarating event.

The clear transitions which John is so careful to provide as he moves into each chronological step within a vision can become a problem, particularly in relation to analysis of organization and climaxes. In the vision of the opening of the sealed scroll, for example, it is important to consider the vision as a minor unit of the whole that begins with 4:1 and ends with 8:5, with its thunder, lightning, and earthquake. Chapter 4 is the introduction and the action really begins with the first mention of the scroll in 5:1. Chapter 6 begins the series of breaking the seals. This moves fairly rapidly until we come to the sixth seal. Each small episode has its own minor climax and all but the first are set off by direct discourse. This inserted dialogue, brief though it is, must be done in each case with some attention to character and situation, whether the cry or song comes from the assembled angels or from the horsemen. There are even some stage directions such as "shout in a voice like thunder" (6:10, The Jerusalem Bible) which must not be ignored. The climax of the action—the whole vision—comes with the great day of vengeance, and there is a very skillful use of suspense and cause and effect during the giving of the seal to those who had served God. This latter section, chapter 7, is the climax upon which hope of salvation depends, and its intensity must not be allowed to suffer in contrast with the more spectacular units of vengeance and destruction. The breaking of the seventh seal is the conclusion or the denouement, but it is emphasized by the sudden silence and leads neatly into the next major unit with the mention of the trumpets.

The second episode of the angels with their trumpets follows much the same pattern as the vision of the sealed scrolls, with another effective suspense mechanism: "That was the first of the troubles; there are still two more to come" (Rev. 8:12, The Jerusalem Bible).

There is an interesting shift in point of view at the beginning of chapter 10 which was hinted at but not developed as early as 4:1 and 5:5 where first a voice speaks directly to John, drawing him into the assembly, and later an elder addresses him individually. In chapter 10 he is visited by an angel and cautioned against revealing certain things, while being told that he may reveal others. Then he is given a kind of measuring rod and becomes an active participant in the events that follow.

For the next two visions (12:1–16:21) the narrator returns to his role of spectator and auditor with frequent uses of "Then I Saw" and "I heard." Chapters 14 and 15, which are the vision of the end of the world, are particularly rich in auditory imagery and in specific directions for how the direct discourse went. The narrator is again actively drawn into the proceedings in chapter 17, where he remains through 18:11, after which there is a brief return to a distancing between vision and narrator, and finally there are the intimate and active sections on which the Book closes. An awareness of this rhythm of involvement and distancing will do much to allow each unit to operate at its own level of intensity as well as help to build the climaxes within it.

The syntax of Revelation tends to be complex, with numerous descriptive clauses, colons, and semicolons that allow the attributes of many various objects and sounds to be crowded together into one sentence. The sentences are long and involved, and care must be taken that speech phrases and rhetorical emphasis are properly used so that the listeners have time to group the appropriate parts of the sentences together. There are numerous short, simple sentences which often come at the time of the transitions or within the direct discourse, and they provide helpful contrast as well as allowing relief from the crowding descriptions.

On a first reading, The Book of Revelation seems to be almost overly rich in all types of imagery. In reality it is primarily visual and auditory. Things are reported as seen and heard. It must not be forgotten, though, that such sights and sounds will have a profound effect on muscle response and it is here that the interpreter will find his greatest sources of inspiration. The sights are brilliant and magnificent and at the same time astonishing and terrifying in their majesty and scope. The richness of colors, the brightness of jewels, the sounds of thunder, and the flashes of lightning are followed almost immediately by the appearance of the four animals with the unnatural features and the multiplicity of eyes. Very quickly we have the contrasting sight of the Lamb. This is not the docile animal of the flock that we are accustomed to in the New Testament, but rather one that has been sacrificed and has seven horns and seven eyes and whose symbolic meaning is immediately explained so that we are left with no doubt as to the reason for the capitalization of Lamb. The device of capitalization can be suggested in oral performance by this traditional name for Jesus Christ.

The scenes take place against a background of loud voices which echo through vast spaces: "the sound of an immense number of angels," the shouting, singing, crying of "all living things in creation," voices like thunder and the trumpets of angels. The sound builds to the breaking of the seventh seal, which is followed by the startling and effective "silence in heaven for about half an hour" (Rev. 8:1, The Jerusalem Bible), which may have been nothing in the span of eternity but which seems to us mortals as a long silence indeed after all the activity and songs of praise.

Color is used lavishly throughout this Book and the symbolic value of the white, gold, the jewel tones, and the white, red, black, and "deathly pale" horses is immediately clear. The description of the messianic Jerusalem which foreshadows the heavenly Jerusalem is astonishing in its details and precision.

Biblical scholars over the centuries have done much to clarify the allusions and metaphors around which Revelation revolves. It is doubtful whether the interpreter under ordinary circumstances will wish to launch into an elaborate explanation of them before he begins to read, although in some cases it might be appropriate to mention a few of the beast images. The references to the Lamb are probably quite clear in the Christian concept of the Lamb of God. It is interesting to note, however, that like most other metaphors in the New Testament, the root of the allusion is deeply imbedded in the Old Testament. The Jewish apocalyptic writing speaks of a conquering lamb that will destroy the evil of the world and of a horned bull which turns into a lamb with black horns. There is also, of course, the relationship between the lamb and the Passover, as well as the Paschal and Pentecostal lambs.

The beast is Rome on the simplest level, but it can also be amplified to include all persecutors. The dragon and the serpent of Genesis 3:15 are both symbolic of Satan and it will be helpful to recall the references in Genesis 3:15 to the offspring of Eve and the offspring of the serpent being forever at war with each other. One is reminded that John of the Gospels is the only one who depicts the scene of Mary at the foot of the cross wherein Jesus gives her into the care of "the disciple he loved," having first said to her, "Woman, this is your son" (John 19:27, The Jerusalem Bible).

The Book of Revelation can make very exciting and moving oral reading. It seems to be somewhat neglected in modern times, perhaps because in our century we are afraid of emotions and do not respond easily with delight or astonishment and wonder. Perhaps it is because too often Revelation is considered to be a series of horrors, with much being made of its famous horsemen. Taken as a whole, however, it is rooted in unchanging realities, however expressed symbolically, to which faith is always open. It is a dramatic restatement of the belief which has persisted since Exodus that God would be with "his people." From the setting of the seal on the elect we know that for those who have lived according to his laws all is not lost and that the goal is not a new earth but rather a gathering of souls into their heavenly home. Revelation is based on the principle of contrasts and the thunder bolts and fire must be kept in careful balance with the setting of the seal, the hymns of praise, and the bright lights of glory.

The Book of Revelation may make some modern theologians cringe at the naïveté of this picture, but it makes exciting listening and reading. It is a spectacular in larger-than-living color told by one who saw and heard it first-hand. It is an immense panorama of color, sound, and activity, with sections of almost frightening relevance for our own troubled times. Like the Old Testament prophecies, it must be interpreted as a document written by one who was under divine directive to share his experiences with the people.

Index

Aaron, confronts Moses, 26
Acrostic structure, Psalm 111, 164
Action, narrative, 89–90, 93
  climax of, 90–91, 103–105
Acts, Book of, 92, 124–125
Adjectives, 67
Adverbs, 67
Ahasuerus, 49, 100
Alliteration, 73, 149
Allusions, unfamiliar, 6, 73
Alphabetical organization
  Lamentations, Poem III, 172
  Psalms 119 and 145, 164
Amos, 176, 177, 178, 179
Anapest, 153, 156, 157, 162
Anchor Bible:
  Lamentations, 166, 168–174
  Passion and death, 119–124
Andrew, 115
Annas, 120
Antithetic parallelism, 151–152, 159
Articulation, 35
  pronunciation distinguished, 42–43
Assonance, 73
Audience:
  attention of, 7

of Epistles, 139–140
intended, 5
knowledge of, 6, 116–117, 140
response, 24–25
sharing with, 9, 95
Auditory imagery, 26, 188, 189
Authors:
  Lamentations, 167
  Psalms, 147
  purpose, 9–10

Balancing, parallelism, 68
Bible:
  descriptions in, 92–93
  dialogue in, 100–101, 105, 109
  folklore, 84
  imagery in, 26–27
  literary forms of, 7
  poetry in, 141–165
Biography, history as, 98
Bodily action, 17
  gesture and, 21
  habitual, 22–23
Body, interpreter, 14–27
  gestures, 16–17, 21–23
  muscle tone, 20–21
  posture, 16, 18–19, 20, 30–31
  using, 16–17

Body, literary element, 51–52
Breath control, 28–33
   exercises, 30–33, 43
   posture and, 18, 30–31
Browning, Robert, 87

Caiaphas, 120, 121
"Central intelligence," 87–88
Characters, in narratives, 93–95
   Old Testament, 98–102
Chronicles, Books of, 83
Classical period:
   Old Testament, 97
   prophecy, 176
Clauses, 67
Climax:
   narrative, 90–91, 93, 103–105
   Passion, 118–124
   in poetry, 145–146
   prophetic writing, 182
   tension and, 90
Color, use of, 190
Communication, factors of, 3
Complex sentences, 54, 115
Conclusion, literary element, 52–53
   Epistles, 133–134
Connectives, 112
Connotative association, 11–12, 39, 72, 73, 92, 148
Consonance, 73
Consonants, 44
Content, emotive/logical, 11–13
Corinthians:
   Book 1, 49–50, 54–55, 68, 127–130, 133–135
   Book 2, 130
Crisis, climax of action, 90, 146

Dactyl, 153
Daniel, Book of, 98, 182
David, 83
Declarative sentences, 54

Descriptive history, 98
Dialogue, 100–101, 105, 109
Didactic history, 98

Ecclesiastes, Book of, 151–152, 159, 160–163
Elias, 83
Eliphaz, speech to Job, 26–27
Elocutio, 2
Emblematic parallelism, 152
Emotive content, 11–13
   poetry, 142
Empathy, 23–25, 41, 85, 95, 149
   imitative aspect, 25
Epistles, 126–140, 175
   audience of, 139–140
   style of, 133–138
Esther, Book of, 49, 100
   conclusions to, 52–53
Exclamations, 55–56
Exercises:
   for breath control, 30–33, 43
   projection focus, 36–37
Exhalation, 28, 43
   process, 28–29
Exodus, Book of, 83
Ezekiel, 181, 185

Figures of speech, 73–74, 170, 181
Flood, story of the, 105–109
Foot, rhythmic, 153
Foot prosody, 154, 156
Fragments, use of, 6, 10
Fricative sounds, 44–45
Fulcrum, 146, 150

Galatians, Book of, 130–131
Genesis, Book of, 83, 99
   translational comparison, 1, 57–63, 64–66, 68, 73, 78–79, 80
Gestures, 16–17, 21–23, 99

defined, 21
habitual, 22–23
God (*see also* Yahweh):
attitudes of, 100
Hebrew concept of, 104
in New Testament, 114
prophets and, 183
voice of, 99
Gospels, 10, 110, 111–113

Haman, 100
Hebrews:
concept of God, 104
linear concept of history, 91,
98
poetry of, 67–68, 151, 153–
154, 167
Hillers, Delbert R., 166, 167,
168, 171, 172, 173
History:
Hebrew concept of, 91, 98
types of, 97–98
Hosea, 176, 179

Iamb, 153, 156, 157, 162
Imperative sentences, 55
Inflection, 38
Inflection range, 38
Inhalation, process, 28–29
Intelligibility, 42–45
Interpretation:
as art, 7–11
basics of, 1–13
connotations, 1
Interpreter:
attitude of, 20
and audience, 8–9, 95
use of body, 14–27
and character development,
95
as communicator, 3–4
concerns of, 1–2, 13, 46
Epistles, 126–127

and interpretation, 7–11
and literary style, 46–47
as a medium, 14
Passion of Jesus, 119
and phrasing, 78
problems for, 138–140
and translations, 5
use of voice, 27–45
Interrogative sentences, 54–55
Introduction, literary element,
48–51
lead-in sentence as, 48, 50
Inventio, 2
Isaiah, 176, 180–181

James, Book of, 138
James, Henry, 87
Jeremiah, 167, 177, 181
Jerusalem Bible:
Ecclesiastes 3:1–8, 159, 160–
161
Genesis 1, 62–63, 66, 73, 78–
79
Lamentations, 168
Psalm 8, 157–158
Jesus, 10, 48, 113
miracle of loaves and fishes,
114–116
Passion and death, 90, 118–
124
reference to in Gospels, 110,
111–112
speech of, 114, 116–117
Job:
Eliphaz's speech to, 26–27
God speaks to, 100
John, 88, 112–113, 116, 118–
120, 123, 142–143, 185
Book of, 112–113, 115
John (Book of Revelation), 185,
187, 190
Jonah:
Book of, 100

God's attitude toward, 100, 101–102, 105
Joseph, story of, 90, 94, 104–105
  narrator of, 88
Joshua, Book of, 181
Journeys, meaning of, 93
Judas, 119
Jude, Book of, 51–52
Judges, Book of, 181
  simile in, 76

Kinesthetic imagery, 26, 75, 93, 169, 183
Kinetic imagery, 26, 75, 93, 169, 183
King James translation:
  Ecclesiastes 3:1–8, 159
  Genesis 1, 57–60, 64, 66, 73, 79, 80
  prose form, 141
  Psalm 8, 145, 155–156
Kings, Book of, 83, 98, 181
  narrator of, 88
Klang, 39

Lamb, image of the, 189, 190
Lamentations, Book of, 147, 166 –174
  Poem I, 168–170
  Poem II, 170–172
  Poem III, 172–173
  Poem IV, 173–174
Language:
  nonverbal, 3–4, 16–17
  spoken, 3–4
Law, Jewish, 121
Lead-in sentences, 48, 50, 54–55
Lines, poetry, 153
  feminine endings, 144, 163, 172
  length, 162
  masculine endings, 144, 163
Literary analysis, 5

and translations, 48
Logical content, 11–13
  poetry, 143
Luke, 88, 92, 112, 118, 123, 141
  Book of, 112, 115
Lysimachus, 53

McLuhan, Marshall, 12
Mark, 88, 112, 115, 118, 123, 142
  Book of, 112, 115
Matthew, 88, 111, 115, 118, 123, 142
  Book of, 48, 111–112, 115
Meaning, 4–7
Message:
  effect of, 9
  experience as, 3
  purpose, 9–10
Metaphor, 73–74, 144–145, 168, 169, 172, 190
Micah, 176, 180
Mood, 39
Moses, 181
  and Aaron, 26
Munck, Johannes, 124
Muscle tone, 20–21, 85, 95

Narratives, 83–96
  action, 89–90
  body of, 51–52
  characters in, 93–95
  climax, 90–91
  conclusion, 52
  defined, 84
  narrator and, 85–87
  in New Testament, 110–125, 185
  in Old Testament, 97–109
  oral tradition and, 84–85, 91
  place, 91–93
  plot, 89–90
  style, 105–109

time, 91–93
types, 113–116
Narrator:
  and characters, 94
  point of view, 87–88
  problems of, 116–118
  sharing experience related, 85
    –87
New English Bible:
  Ecclesiastes 3:1–8, 159, 161–
    163
  Lamentations, 169
  Psalm 8, 145, 149–150
New Testament:
  parables, 48
  poetry in, 142–143
  similes in, 75, 77
Noah, story of, 105–109
Nouns, 67

Object, 67
Old Testament:
  humor in, 100, 101–102
  narratives in, 49, 84–85, 97–
    109
  periods, 97
  poetry in, 143
  similes in, 74–75
Onomatopoeia, 73
Oral tradition, and narratives,
    84–85, 91
Organization, poetry, 145–148

Pace, monotony of, 6–7
Parables, 48
  activity of, 89
  point of view, 88
Parallelism, 67–70, 78, 107, 138
  in poetry, 150, 151–152, 154,
    162
  and stresses, 80
  types, 151–152

Passion and death, Jesus', 118–
  124
Paul, 139, 143
  first letter to Corinthians, 49–
    50, 54–55, 68, 127–130,
    133–135
  second letter to Corinthians,
    130
  letter to the Galatians, 130–
    131
  letter to the Romans, 51, 130–
    132
  letters to Timothy, 128, 133,
    134, 136–137
  letter to Titus, 133, 135, 137
Pauses, 41, 55
  poetry, 153
Persona, 147, 155, 168–169, 171,
    172, 175, 184
Personification, 73, 144–145
Perspective, 87–88
Peter, 112, 120
Philip, 115
Phrases, speech, 67, 77–79
Pilate, 121–122
Pitch, 37–40
  change of, 38
  defined, 38
  monotony of, 6–7
Place, narrative, 91–93, 112
Plosives, 44
Plot, narrative, 89–90
  climax of, 90–91, 103–105
Poetry:
  defined, 141
  effect of translation on, 148,
    154
  Hebrew, 67–68, 151, 153–
    154, 167
  organization, 145–148
  parallelism in, 150, 151–152,
    154, 162

prophecies, 176, 178–179, 180
rhythm, 153–165
style, 144–145
types, 146–147
word choice, 148–150
Point of view, narration, 87–88
Posture, 16, 18–19, 20, 95
and breath control, 18, 30–31
defined, 18
Practice, 15–16
breathing exercises, 30–33, 43
projection focus, 36–37
reading aloud, 14–15, 138, 144
Prodigal Son, parable of, 91
Projection, 33–35, 85
faulty, 43
focus of, 35–37
Pronouns, 67
possessive, 93
Pronunciatio, 2–3
Pronunciation, 35
articulation distinguished, 42 –43
guides to, 43
Prophecy, tradition of, 176
Prophetic writings, 92, 175–184
Prosody, 154, 167
Proverbs, Book of, 152
simile in, 76
Psalms, Book of, 146–147, 164
8th, 145, 149–150, 155–158
23rd, 146
Public address systems, 34
Punctuation:
handling, 70, 188–189
and phrasing, 78
and rate, 41–42
translation and, 56, 70
Purpose:
author's, 9–10
clarifying, 10
Pyrrhic, 153

Quality, voice, 39–40
defined, 39
Questions, 54–55
rhetorical, 54, 131

Rate, 40–42
Reader (*see* Interpreter)
References, archaic, 6, 72, 76
References, geographic, 6, 92–93
Reuben, as a character, 94
Revelation, Book of, 185–191
Rhetorical questions, 54, 131
Rhythm:
poetry, 153–165
prose, 79–83, 131, 135–136, 137, 188
Romans, Book of, 51, 130–132
Romantic period, Old Testament, 97
Ruth, Book of, 100–101

Salutation, 133, 134, 186
Samuel, Book of, 83, 99–100, 181
Scientific history, 98
Sense imagery, 26–27, 183
types, 26
Sentences:
lead-in, 48, 50, 54–55
length, 57–66, 115, 131, 136, 144, 188–189
in poetry, 144
structure, 53–56
syntax, 67–71, 115
types, 54–55
word order, 56
Setting, 102
Simile, 73–74, 169, 172

in New Testament, 75, 77
in Old Testament, 74–75, 76, 144–145
Simple sentences, 54
Song of Songs, 145, 147
Sower, parable of the, 117
Spondee, 153
Stress prosody, 154
Stresses:
  Genesis 1, 80–81
  phrases, 80, 136–137
  poetry, 153–154, 156–157, 158, 179
Style, literary, 46–82
  body, 51–52
  conclusion, 52–53
  elements, 47
  Epistles, 133–138
  introduction, 48–51
  Old Testament narrative, 105–109
  phrasing, 77–79
  poetry, 144–145
  prophetic writing, 183–184
  prose rhythm, 79–83
  sentence structure, 53–71
  shifts in, 107, 118
  word choice, 71–77
Subject, sentence, 67
Suspense, 118, 188
Syllabic prosody, 154
Symbolism, 112, 187
Symbols, written, 3–4
  influences, 4
Synonymous parallelism, 151
Synoptic Gospels, 10, 111
Syntax, 67–71, 77
  Hebrew, 102
  poetry, 144
  Revelation, 188–189
Synthetic parallelism, 152

Sypherd, W. O., 151, 153

Teaching narrative, 113
Technique, 15–16
Tense, 112, 171
  Hebraic language, 103
Timbre, 39
Time, narrative, 91–93, 112
Timothy, Books of, 128, 133, 134, 136–137
Titus, Book of, 133, 135, 137
Tone color, 73, 149, 150, 170
Torah, Genesis 1, 60–62, 64–66, 68, 73, 79
Translations:
  conformity among, 70–71
  poetry and, 148, 154
  problems of, 2, 5, 9
  punctuation, 56, 70
  and rhythm, 82
  and style, 48
Trochee, 153

Vashti, Queen, 49
Verbs, 67
Visual imagery, 26, 181, 189
Voice, improving, 27–45
  breath control, 18, 28–33
  pitch, 37–40
  projection, 33–37
  quality, 37–40
  rate, 40–42
  volume, 33–35
Volume, 33–35

Word choice, 71–77, 134–135
  poetry, 148–150

Yahweh, 103, 104, 184

Zechariah, 185